JUST ANOTHER HONEYMOON IN FRANCE

~ A Vagabond at Large ~

NATHAN BROWN

MEZCALITA
PRESS

D0897197

FIRST EDITION
Copyright © 2019 by Nathan Brown
All Rights Reserved
ISBN-13: 978-0-9994784-7-9

Library of Congress Control Number:
2019911215

No part of this book may be performed,
recorded, thieved, or otherwise trans-mitted
without the written consent of the author
and the permission of the publisher.
However, portions may be cited for book
reviews—favorable or otherwise—without
obtaining consent.

Cover Design: Chris Everett

MEZCALITA PRESS, LLC
Norman, Oklahoma

JUST ANOTHER HONEYMOON IN FRANCE

~ A Vagabond at Large ~

NATHAN BROWN

ALSO BY NATHAN BROWN

TABLE OF CONTENTS

ACKNOWLEDGEMENTS

First, Ashley… thank you for marrying me. Thank you for still being here. And thank you for seeming to be okay with all the things my books reveal about our life.

Lise Liddell, your beautiful friendship and extraordinary generosity made this trip possible. Thank you, Lise. Really.

Chip & Janet, Sandra & Jack, many thanks for the same.

Chris Everett, your fantastic eye and long-vision have made my book covers memorable for years. And this series looks to be our best effort yet!

The good fortune of a lifetime of travel I owe to my parents, Lavonn and Norma. They've supported me for over 50 years now through the decades and antics of a struggling artist. A term we should go ahead and just make one word.

INTRODUCTION

Just Another Honeymoon in France marks the beginning of my venture into travel memoir. A genre I've been writing for decades, but haven't published until now. So this is the first in a series of books about a life spent on the road called "A Vagabond at Large."

The scenes and events here are based on reality. At the same time, Ashley may remember some of what happened a bit differently. In defense of us both, though, it was our honeymoon, and so, the champagne and wine were certainly flowing.

JUST ANOTHER HONEYMOON IN FRANCE

NATHAN BROWN

Just Another American Idiot

In the cloudy and humid mug of early May, I prepare for our upcoming trip with *The Pocket Idiot's Guide to French*. It promises "Idiot-proof steps" and to help me "Grapple with grammar and win." The first claim I find insulting. And the second, quite lofty.

At the same time, when a man in his forties has lived most of his life in Oklahoma and then, one day, finds himself preparing to leave for France on a honeymoon with his beautiful new wife from Houston, what other book would he use? Besides, in the early pages of the pronunciation guide, the author offers some downright sound advice to beginning poets, as well as everyday doofuses interested in learning French:

> Do not overemphasize letters, words, or syllables. This will target you as a novice and will ruin the sounds of the language.

My sentiments exactly. And with a bit of further introspection, one can also sense in these words the root system that nurtures an internationally uniform disdain, if not disgust, for the sadly prolific subspecies of:

Eye-rollus Americanus

...the American Tourist.

Raison du Voyage

This at the start of endearing years
I recall the earth loved us a little.

~ René Char, "Évadné"

This journey begins on two wheels...
the two rings Ashley and I exchanged at
sunset last Saturday night in a backyard
strewn with rose petals, just up the hill
from Lake Travis near Austin. The road
to get here, though, was a long one that
required a good deal of driving it.

I'd taken an eleven-and-a-half-year
sabbatical from marriage. As the key
Defendant in Case No. FD-99-Yada-

and-Yada, I was slow to pick up on the court's inside jokes about the process of divorce and custody in Oklahoma. One of the big ones is that, if you have the Y chromosome, you will pay. There are more. But I am already dancing on a libelous edge here. So let's just say that by the time the notary stamped that sad decree, matrimony as an institution had lost a lot of its shine for me.

Nonetheless, a few years out from it—since I am a male and still harbor the problematic hormones that go with it—I decided to give dating a whirl and was soon blessed with a few wonderfully romantic disasters. Each one, its own sexy and unique version of hell. So, I began to think what many guys begin to think at the end of that fourth, or was it fifth, gloriously amorous failure. I'm done.

I waved that brave and delusional flag for a year or so. Even got pretty cocky with it. And then—as often happens when a person takes all systems offline and powers down—came my Ashley... who was, when we met four years ago, at the frayed tail end of her own little wonderfully romantic disaster.

As chance loves to have it, the Austin songwriter Jimmy LaFave introduced us at the huge International Folk Alliance Conference in Memphis. And it was there, in a dingy hotel lobby, with an even dingier hotel carpet, that we exchanged guarded niceties, laughed a little over the collective psychosis of such a gathering of folk musicians, and then decided to get together that night for bad ten-dollar margaritas in the hotel bar. The margaritas arrived in Styrofoam coffee cups, because the bartender was out of glasses. Still, we tapped them together in the muted thud of a toast that knocked off the pathetic amount of salt he tried to put on them, smiled, and then agreed that, yes, they were really bad.

The rest of the story already has quite a few songs and poems written about it. So I'll do my best to bring things back around to last Saturday night. The hot summer before, and over considerably better margaritas in Santa Fe's lovely La Fonda hotel, she had said "Yes" to my marriage proposal. Much to the relief of my parents. And to the notable concern of hers. Ten months later, we sealed the holy deal at her father and stepmother's beautiful house on the lake.

And that is what brings us to the foot of this trip to France. A honeymoon, they call it. A word I should understand better than I do if I'm to spend a week or two over among the shadows of all that love and light we keep crediting to the French and their capital city.

VIVE LA TEQUILA

Speaking of tequila, here on this early summer evening in the Texas Hills, I'm on our couch slowly sipping down a second margarita in preparation for

THE GREAT GALLIC TEQUILA DROUGHT OF 2011

—a dry weather pattern I know will set in the moment the plane lands in Paris.

Ashley shakes up one of the best salty concoctions in the Southwest. And, you'd have a problem like mine if you ever tasted one. But when I reflect on my abysmal attempts to obtain a good 'rita over in Greece a few years ago—

9

even when carefully walking the willing bartender at Athinaion Politeia through the process there in the shadow of the Acropolis—I have resigned myself to the likelihood that there is not one to be had on the European continent.

That said, even Okies have heard tell that the wine in France is downright passable, if not outright exceptional, considerin' how long they've been at it over there with all o' them green and purple grapes n' all. Someone also told me the Trappist monks there are quite skilled with fermentatin' the hops n' the barley n' such. Though, as a recoverin' Southern Baptist preacher's kid, I can't imagine men o' the cloth ever touchin' the stuff.

By the way, if you think I'm going to keep it up with that horrendous and stereotypical -in' thing? Please... put your fear to rest.

No Equivalent

The French "r" requires the
participation of your throat.

~ Gail Stein,
The Pocket Idiot's Guide to French

Again, such poetic advice from Ms.
Stein. And it's true that, outside of
overall vocabulary, few things require
more exercise and preparation before a
trip to France than achieving a halfway
acceptable pronunciation of the letter *r*
in *le français*. Of course, so few things
are acceptable to the French anyway—
especially to their waiters. Like, for
example, your choice of the wrong-

colored wine to go with the medium-cooked chateaubriand that he'd clearly suggested *should* be medium-rare. So, it's a waste of energy to worry too much about it. At the same time, some of the other folks over there, who are not said waiters, I've heard will at least pretend to appreciate your linguistic efforts and smile, while half nodding. Even if they do it with a look of polite continental pity.

But Ms. Stein does give some excellent pointers in her book on positioning the tongue and shaping the sound. So, in an effort to avoid redundancy, I will add only this one simple exercise, merely as a compliment to her good counsel: The French *r* is something like gargling with cognac—a tad potent, and somewhat uncomfortable at first. But, the reward is coming. For best results, I suggest gargling small amounts several times throughout the afternoon. Swallowing after each. This way, when you get to the restaurant, that mean old waiter will have little effect on your ability to go ahead and enjoy the exquisite dull glow of the streetlamps there on the table-strewn sidewalk in the Latin Quarter. Who knows, he might even be humbled by his inability to beat you into culinary submission. But don't bet on it.

No Words

It's a plane ride over Upstate New York, where storms are bringing a taste of Noah's plight to the Northeast. And the bump and grind of turbulence up here at 31,000 feet tells us all we need to know about what's going on down there.

It's also a single-serving Pepperidge Farm Milano cookie between sips of this tepid and powdered decaf coffee— a lukewarm concoction that is just awful beyond the amount of time I'm willing to sacrifice trying to describe just how awful it is.

But it is very much a beginning to a honeymoon, that is also a beginning to a marriage—a marriage to a wonderful woman who is asleep next to me here in seat 27K.

And it has taken me so long to write this one little journal entry, we're almost to Halifax now. But it's only because I can't quite find the words to tell you just how wonderful and beautiful she really is… how sweet she is, compared to this cup of coffee… and how good she is to, and for, me.

And yet, now that I've had a few bites, this little Milano cookie's pretty darn good too.

MERDE DU PIGEON

The taxi ride from Charles de Gaulle
Airport into the Latin Quarter reminds
me that all great cities—even this one
that claims to be made of love and
light—have their "other sides," made of
dirt and grime, warehouses and steel
yards. And that all crosstown trips from
dingy gray airports into the veins and
heart of where you want to be will be
fraught with honking horns, lane-
choking construction work, and
beaucoup traffic.

And that even when you get there, drag
your luggage up to the fifth-floor room,
then set out for that first romantic stroll

along the River Seine, you will still have to step over some trash and pigeon shit now and then on the cracked curbs and skinny little Parisian sidewalks.

Yet, somehow, every bit of it will manage to be miraculous.

LUNE DE MIEL

Paris + Honeymoon = a lot of pressure
on a 46-year-old guy who *loves* to travel
and *lives* to journal about it. Meaning,
he's invested a good number of years in
the market of making everything—from
where to eat and how long to sit there,
to where to go hang out afterwards and
grab some coffee while he writes down
the experiences—all about him and
what he'd rather do next.

Thus, here on this unique occasion, he
works the careful algebra (upon arrival
at l'hotel) of sneaking downstairs and
ordering a half bottle of champagne to
be brought up to the room while the

one-he-does-not-want-to-lose is showering—sort of like a bubbly preemptive strike against all those mistakes he will inevitably make over the next week or two when he forgets his new *raison du vivre*.

Just like the one he's making right now, after placing that order, with these few bites of café éclair and a porcelain cup of steaming coffee at a white-laced window table in the dining room of the Hotel Dauphine – St. Germain.

REVERIES

a big city designed to trouble the
mind of the most impervious
solitary.

~ Baudelaire on Paris
"A Wag" *Paris Spleen*

① *These French*

Not to overplay it, but walking through
the Jardin du Luxembourg earlier today
around lunchtime—which in Paris is
roughly between noon and 6:00 p.m.—
so many people, ranging in ages from
late teens to early 70s, were... and I'm

not sure how to make my point here,
but, they were... reading books. Or
they were lying on benches, holding
hands and eating baguette sandwiches
while laughing and talking about life
and which rosé they should buy at the
corner store.

Two middle-aged Japanese men in dark
blue suits were the only ones texting or
staring at their cell phones. No one else.
And there were hundreds of people. I
mean, really? What is wrong with these
French? All this smiling, sitting in the
sunshine, reading books, and other rot?

② *What the Guide Book
Won't Tell You*

If you weigh over 180 pounds, do not
plan on using a public restroom in this
town. Every restaurant we've eaten in
so far, when it comes time for a quick
powder, involves either a dizzying set of

spiraling stairs or a claustrophobic stall that is the size of a red London phone booth. Or both. And one time, when I squeezed in with my backpack, I came damn close to never coming out again. I had to put the lid down, stand on the toilet, open the door, which of course opened inward, then jump out while holding my pack behind me.

I'm not trying to offend the French Public Authority. I'm simply trying to spare the football players and fast-food eaters of the world the trouble.

③ *In Paris...*

Girls will...

wear short skirts with no pantyhose on cold mornings; they'll sport high heels, of the six-inch variety, on mopeds and scooters; and they will walk tiny dogs on studded black-leather leashes while reading hardback books from behind extraordinarily large and sexy black sunglasses.

Guys will...

wear multiple scarves piled so high they appear to prop up their heads; and they will ride bicycles in white shorts while smoking cigarettes with their left hands and gripping tennis racquets under a right armpit—sometimes with hair long enough to blow all Fabio-like in the Parisian breeze.

And neither, under any circumstances, will...

yield to you on the sidewalks of the Champs-Élysées. You can move out of their way... or take your chances.

Reflections. . .
or maybe just thoughts. . .
on Hemingway

Then there was the bad weather.

~ opening line of *A Moveable Feast*

I've never been long on literary idol worship. But the writers I love—the ones who make me feel like I'm stealing a King-Sized Butterfinger candy bar from a gas station every time I pick up one of their books—I tend to get a bit geeky about. These would include Bukowski and Baudelaire, Stephen Dunn, Tony Hoagland, Dostoyevsky, and, I don't know… maybe Pablo Neruda. And, lyrically speaking, I think I might ask Sting to marry me if I ever met him. And yes, my wife knows this.

It also seems like Hemingway got through to me once or twice, long ago. *For Whom the Bell Tolls*, *The Old Man and the Sea*. And that's why I decided to wrap up in the warm cliché of reading again his memoir, *A Moveable Feast*, on this trip. I know. I couldn't help it. But keep in mind, I just bought a copy of Céline's *Journey to the End of the Night* at the notorious bookstore Shakespeare and Company on the rue de la Bûcherie along the Seine. So I'll be getting back to my old sardonic self soon enough.

> Do not worry. You have always written before and you will write now. All you have to do is write one true sentence. Write the truest sentence that you know.
>
> ~ *A Moveable Feast*

I'm a fourth of the way in. And I'm enjoying it. It makes me want to write shorter, and truer, sentences. It makes me want to work every morning. It makes me want to write in coffee shops and cafés. However, I'm not sure… well, I'll just say it: I don't really think the book is all that, necessarily, good.

So he walked down the rue to the river, turned toward Notre Dame. He saw the fishermen. Commented on them. Then he crossed over to visit a favorite book vendor. Talked to her about books for a while. And then he went back to the flat on Cardinal Lemoine and told Hadley all about it.

And I know he's Hemingway and all. And there are definitely some one-line zingers here and there. Like on page 49:

> The only thing that could spoil a day was people and if you could keep away from making

engagements, each day had no
limits. People were always the
limiters of happiness except for the
very few that were as good as
spring itself.

Okay, so that was two lines. And I
know I need to keep reading further.
But I'm beginning to wonder if it is
possible to write one true sentence too
many.

BAR HEMINGWAY

I'll come back to his book later. Right
now, I'd like to mention when and
where Hemingway met me more than
halfway.

A friend of mine in Dallas comes to
Paris more often than I do, which
wouldn't take much, and he told me I
should check out Bar Hemingway at
Hôtel Ritz. And, since there would at
least be a bar at the end of the line, this
seemed like a no-miss situation.

We burned a lot of shoe rubber trying
to find the place. And then, when we
did finally locate Place Vendôme, we

made the mistake of walking up to the main entrance of the Ritz. Here, we were almost-politely "rescued" by a gold-trimmed valet who appeared most concerned with the state and status of our travel attire. We asked about the possibility of exploring some of the hotel… maybe the restaurant? *Clos-éd.* Maybe the bar? *Réservé.* I thought about explaining that I was a rather famous American author but realized that the French would consider that to be an oxymoron. And then, we have the problem that it isn't true. So, out of total desperation, I asked about Bar Hemingway?

Awh! Oui, oui, monsieur. He gestured in French that we must exit the way we came in, go all the way around the block to the back of the hotel, and that we would find it at 38 Rue Cambon. He seemed both pleased to help, and quite relieved we would soon be gone.

It's no short walk around the Ritz Paris. But we made it... to the closed and locked door. We gathered from other information the valet had given us in French that Bar Hemingway didn't open until 6:30. We were ten minutes early. And so, refusing to give up after all the effort and humiliation, we sat down on a stone ledge along the sidewalk and waited. While there, I noticed a wolf in chef's clothing squatting by the curb and smoking. And we both noticed, because he was so indiscreetly noticeable, a gentleman, with a bald head and sunglasses that made him look like a German architect, who was pacing the sidewalk in front of us in purple suede moccasins, a collared lilac shirt, and a thick bunched-up scarf of a slightly lighter shade of lilac. He puffed on a cigarette and kept looking at his watch with an air of impatience while glancing over at the door to the bar every thirty seconds or so.

At 6:32, we stepped in and were greeted
by the first kind waitress we'd encountered in Paris. Actually, she was the only.
Other waitpersons had tolerated us
better than others. But this girl smiled,
let us choose a table—the best in the
place—and brought us three small
bowls of bar treats before we even had
a chance to open our menus.

That last move on her part played a
critical role in our decision to stay put.
Because, after we opened the menus,
we saw that there was no drink listed
for less than 30 Euros. My old English
major math skills warned me that this
comes out, at the current exchange rate,
to somewhere around 48 dollars. Poets
are capable of making this one narrowly
focused type of calculation, because it's
critical to always know just how much

money they do not have at any given time. So, needless to say, a lump shot up in my throat. We stared back and forth, eyes wide, and tried to figure out what to do without speaking at audible volumes.

I considered bolting for a second, but then our purple friend from the sidewalk came sashaying in and took a seat at the far end of the bar. I remembered how he'd looked down his aquiline nose at us, the one or two times he'd bothered, and a useless pride took hold of me. I turned back, squinted at Ashley, and asked with my eyes if she was with me on this one. Her eyes seemed to say yes. (I guess I should check with her now to see if I was right about that.) Anyway, we put our fingers to the menu and went to work on a choice... a choice which, I should be honest, also had a big impact on our decision to stay.

The menu made it clear that they take a margarita very seriously. They were listed prominently and came with five choices for salt. I can't remember them all, but we went with a smoked ginger variety. (And it did not disappoint.) However, on the tequilas, they offered only three: Cazadores, Patrón, and Sauza... a selection weak as water, but survivable. In a way, it served as a small amount of vindication though—that the French, for all their snootiness about wine and cheese, appear to verge on ignorance when it comes to tequila. So, I went with the Patrón because the kind waitress recommended it and was still smiling, so I wanted to keep things that way.

She swooshed away with the order, still smiling, and we turned our attention to the bar treats. These were better than some of the meals we'd had. Incredible local olives. A few beautifully presented potato chips. And some kind of candied nuts that somehow involved a hint of peanut butter. To die for.

When the margarita arrived, I'll shoot straight and tell you that they won me over with the presentation. It came in a large classic margarita glass. The color and opacity gave evidence that freshly-squeezed lime juice was an ingredient. No ice. My hopes rose with the glass to my lips. I licked the reddish-brown ginger salt and took a sip.

Now... I did not cry. I want you to know that. Though, there was almost cause to. Not quite. But we were getting unnervingly close. Maybe it was because we were in Paris. Or, because it was Hemingway's bar. Maybe it was because we were half a world away from Jalisco, Mexico—tequila's homeland. Or maybe it was... just that good. But it doesn't matter. Something about the warmth of the wood walls, the brass trim, all the black and white photos of Hemingway from his younger days on up to his varying stages of decay, and the way Ashley was eyeing their famous gin martini, but only did exactly that, because she loves me and knew we could only afford one drink. But… something made the whole thing work.

So there, toward the last few sips, we each took a turn. And then I raised that last one up to the ghost of Ernest, ol' Papa, thanked him for the moment, and promised to read the *Feast* to the end.

P.S. — If you ever try to find this place and come up with the address 15, Place Vendôme on the Internet, don't believe it for a second. This bar's around back.

Table 75

It was a quick walk to Lipp's and
every place I passed that my
stomach noticed as quickly as my
eyes or my nose made the walk
an added Pleasure.

~ Hemingway
A Moveable Feast

After mentioning the cliché of reading
A Moveable Feast, I should mention that
Paris is awash in opportunities for one
to participate in clichés. (French does,
after all, supply English with the term
for the problem.) And if you're staying
in the Latin Quarter, you might as well

resign yourself to the impossibility of avoiding them.

Boulevard Saint Germain is a perfect example. Down in the heart of it are two cafés: Café de Flores and Deux Maggots. A table on the sidewalk at either of these places is the perfect spot for anyone who is of the desperate disposition of wanting, if not dying, to be seen. A glance at all the empty tables *inside*, is proof of this. So, when it came time for dinner on our first night in this city we know almost nothing about, we somehow knew, at the very least, to go with the slightly lesser sin of dining at Brasserie Lipp across the street.

We got a beautiful little two-seater table right by a window on the second floor. The waiter, without being too kind, was pleasant enough and quickly brought out a sleek and classy looking gin martini for Ashley and a glass of Riesling for me. We held a subtle but loving toast to our honeymoon up in the reflection of the window panes and then looked down with a subtle but reserved sense of superiority at all the poor clichés sitting at their sad little tables on the fume-infested sidewalk across Saint Germain.

To top off the experience, the waiter was just French enough to refuse my interest in trying out the andouillette, saying it was too *français* for an *américain*, and so steered me toward the Chateau Filet de Boeuf instead…

…a subtle, but well-deserved adjustment to my brief sense of superiority.

FROM ICI TO LÀ

The trip to Bordeaux harbored few difficulties, which surprised us. The taxi from the hotel to the train station was less traumatic, less time consuming, and much less expensive than the one from the airport. Times and gates were clearly posted. We'd upgraded to "Comfort Class" and it lived up to its name. And the train, according to Lise—our friend whose maison we were headed for—travels at about 180 miles per hour. So, barring a derailment, we'd get where we were going in no time.

The more interesting story from this part of the journey came through the

odd circumstance that poetry happened
to come in handy for a change. I'd just
set a copy of Baudelaire's *Paris Spleen*
out on the table in front of me when
the steward came by with the food
cart—yet another perk of Comfort
Class. He'd thoroughly ignored us up to
that point. But when he saw Baudelaire,
he lit up and asked me if I'd heard of
the Persian poet, Omar Vayom. He
wasn't sure about the spelling. But he
truly liked him… said his main themes
were wine, women, love, and death…
and that the poems were very short.
Sounds good on every count. So for the
rest of our rail-related part of the trip,
we had his persistent smile every time
he walked by and a heightened level of
comfort in our newfound sense of class.

Getting from the train, through the station, then out to and into our Avis rental car, inflicted a mild but expected trauma. Getting the small stick-shift car, of a foreign model and make I'd never seen, out of the lot and onto the A10 was daring but doable. The hour or so on the A10 toll road was, all in all, pleasant and felt a bit like splitting the middle of Oklahoma on I-44.

However, getting off the A10, when you've missed your exit, and then, eventually, back to the house you're hoping to spend the night in, somewhere inside the tiny village of Saint Sauvant, turned out to be something close to Dante's Fifth or Sixth Circle of Hell. And when you are looking to Purgatory for relief, tomorrow has just got to be a better day.

Here's how it went. After missing the exit, I took the next, which spit us onto some other toll road that had no exit. It took some twenty kilometers to reach a toll booth. There, I chose a lane with a monstrous machine, instead of a real person, and this massive metal box spoke only French on its outer parts. And in the thick of this magical little moment is when I discovered the car had no reverse. Not that I could find. The gear-stick knob said it was there. But in all my jerking and thrashing, mashing and cursing, I'm telling you… it wasn't there. Yet, the fact no longer mattered since there were now thrashing and cursing French drivers in line behind us.

Maybe ten yards ahead and to the right were a man and a woman in toll-booth-looking garb talking with their feet up on a guardrail. We screamed for help— "aide" or something. We could not remember. They crinkled their brows, but otherwise made no effort to move. An increase in our volume and a honk from behind finally got them to motion to someone else hidden to our eyes by the big metal monster. Soon, a woman appeared from around the corner of the French-speaking box, startling me, and impatiently fed my ticket and euros to the thin-lipped mouth of the machine that seemed just as angry.

From here on we took two-lane roads with red numbers. And even though we didn't know where we were going, at least we could be lost without being charged for it.

After much winding, round-a-bouting, and map-wrenching, we did make it into the tiny alley with a big name, the Grande Rue des Mottes, that runs in front of Lise's house. It took me only four tries to get the car into the gravel courtyard. And, in the process, I finally discovered the car did, in fact, have a reverse gear. But not without throwing my right shoulder out in the terrible effort.

So yes, there was some trauma, some drama, and a few colorful words, but once we stepped inside of the house— the beautiful maison nestled inside this beautiful little village—the beautiful village nestled inside these beautiful hills of southern France—something began to change.

True. We had no food and no bottled water yet. True. We failed to find the supermarche to which we'd been given careful hand-drawn directions that was back in the main town of Saintes. So, it was also true… breakfast was going to be a bit of a problem.

But we did find La Romana, a quiet Italian restaurant—the only place that appeared to still be open—along the central drag just east of the river. And the owner, or maître d', or garçon—we were never quite sure—managed our English with great skill and brought us two gorgeous green salads in sloping white bowls, then a hot and tasty handmade pizza heavy laden with all kinds of veggies. His spunkiness and wit gave us hope for this new leg of our journey, and we slept like old dogs after a long walk.

SAINT SAUVANT

In her instructions, our friend told us to check out a brand new boutique hotel around the corner and up the hill from the village TABAC. She'd mentioned it had a small bar and we thought that might bring a soft end to a hard day. On the way up to it, a white-haired gentleman in cargo shorts and sandals politely accosted us in French. We tried to explain that we did not understand. Unperturbed, he said, *Awh, Anglais*, then continued on in French but with bigger hand gestures he was sure would help.

We put together bits and pieces. One was that he wanted us to follow him into a small yard behind a moss-covered stone building. This didn't seem too strange, since most of the buildings here are covered in moss and made of stone. He stepped down into a 6 X 8 foot depression, cleared away some weeds, and revealed a small opening in the side of it. He spoke in animated terms with a lot of motion. We made out the word "pain," which fortunately means "bread" in French. And so, we finally figured out he was showing us an ancient oven for baking bread.

We registered our pleasure, as well as some relief, and then tried to ask him about the hotel. And since the word for hotel is "hôtel," things moved along a little faster. He escorted us on up the hill but seemed somewhat concerned, like he wasn't quite sure we would be welcome there. But he brought us around into a small breezeway and introduced us to the owners, who were nice, yet reserved. So, we introduced ourselves. They nodded. Then we said where we were from. They perked up a little. Then we mentioned where we were staying and whose house it was. And at the mention of Lise's name, their faces lit up with a warm glow of acceptance, and we knew we were in.

The short of it is that we had just met Hervé and Florence Audinet. Hervé, another white-haired gentleman, but with black-frame glasses and very kind eyes, it turns out is a well-known, if not fairly famous, French architect. And the Design Hotel serves as more than enough evidence of this. During our tour he told us that seven or so other architects own places in Saint Sauvant and that one or two of those are from Houston no less. Other eye-cocking and amazing things about this petite village would surface over the next few days. But for now, I'll say that our tour ended with a snifter of cognac and a bright blue cocktail called Hpnotiq that is bottled right here in Saint Sauvant and sold by the millions around the world. And we sipped them both on the wooden deck of an immaculate terrace at sunset as we sat at a very chíc silver table with a stone slab top and chain mail for a tablecloth. Yes, chain mail.

And all of this also took place in the immediate shadow of a 2,000-year-old church just across the Rue de la Raison. And I am still buzzed by the way it reflected in the black water of the bijou swimming pool a few feet from our stone table—our table with the, did I mention, chain mail tablecloth?

I swear, it felt like we were attending an opening exhibition for some slick new German artist at some upscale gallery in New York, and that any minute the guy would pop out in all black clothes with a shaved head and black horn-rimmed glasses and begin to exquisitely ignore everyone. Instead, it was our friend who'd showed us the oven that came around the corner of the church. We smiled and gave him two thumbs up. He smiled back and gave us a big wave, in French.

MORNINGS IN PARADISE

We learned that the TABAC is the *centre du culture* in villages this size. Ours is on a tight corner of the miniscule square— a square that's more of a small "L" formed at the joint of Rue du Marche and Grande Rue du Pont. Though I'm not certain about this. Street names change every few feet. But these are the two signs I can see from my little table out front on the sidewalk.

The TABAC sells bread, cigarettes and wine, along with magazines, news- papers, candy and packaged ice cream treats. One jar has an assortment of large marshmallows in various pastels.

However, it also has a four to five-foot hardwood bar that comes close to a sort of elegance that makes up for what it lacks in length. Whether in Paris or a village of a few hundred people, there's no time of day in France that is off limits to plopping your buns down somewhere and sipping your way through a good stiff drink. It makes getting back to work, if you've got any to do, almost a pleasure.

Speaking of buns, within a couple of days Ash and I had created a game for our walks along the rues and roads through the endless streams of small towns in the country: We counted the number of baguettes and bottles of wine almost every person was carrying in a small sack or backpack on their way home. It might be a slight exaggeration to say that it was everyone? But it's not far off. One guy we swear had four or five baguettes tucked under a left arm and three full-sized bottles of wine secured between the fingers of his right hand.

But here at the TABAC, it took me a day or two to get my bearings—to figure out the what's-what, and how to order my *café crème* and that linguistically confusing *Kinder Bueno* chocolate bar with the nougaty center. And how that one tiny table, down at the end of the front patio—the one with an *Orangina* soda ad covering its white enamel top—in the glow of any morning, turns on the spigot of my pen as well, or better, as any Parisien café or favorite coffee shop in the states.

With each new morning, the faces behind the counter lose a little of their distrust, as they move, slowly, toward smiles. Even the regulars, who come in for an espresso and their daily baguette have brightened up their "Bonjeurs" when they see me writing.

Evenings of the Same

Our evenings soon took on habits of
their own. Snack time around 5:00 to
6:00 p.m. filled the air with smells of
cheese and olives, champagne mustard
and bread, pineau and rosé… smells
reminiscent of snack time at home, but
with an exotic accent. We would set a
small coffee table with reclining chairs
out in the courtyard and light candles
beneath the rose vines and evening
shade of the house. And though the
afternoons got hot sometimes, things
cooled off quickly with the slanting of
the sun's light.

We toasted the honeymoon, often more than once per glass. We ate everything from the plate. I licked it, since there is no disposal in the sink. And then we went in to prepare dinner.

Two large glass doors open onto the courtyard, all but creating a *plein air* kitchen and dining table. So the shift to dinnertime was subtle and all of about five feet away from snack time—an incredible conservation of energy. Ashley would boil pasta and slice up veggies from the afternoon run to the market, while sipping on a cook's drink. And sometimes, just to put an edge of home on things, she would pipe in a little Hayes Carll warbling on about Beaumont, Texas and drunken poets. Or maybe the Cowboy Junkies singing about murder in the trailer park, or Townes Van Zandt. I mean, we love it here, but we don't want to totally sell out and start listening to accordions and lounge music all day.

While she cooked, I might sit at the
dining table and write. I say 'might.'
That's a lie. I always did it. (A total
violation of honeymoon statutes that
she tolerated with exceptional grace.)
But when she filled the plates, I cleared
the journals away and lit more candles.
Our glasses went from white to red.
More toasts rang out. The smell of olive
oil and parmesan mingled with the fruit
of the vine. And the evening silences of
the village began to set in.

Quite unlike human holidays, this
is an orgy of silence.

~ Baudelaire
Paris Spleen

To say much more would be sacrilege. But these evenings are beautiful things. Ashley is a very beautiful woman. Saint Sauvant is a magical, if not a sacred, place. And this kind of quiet is a balm and bandage for the wayfaring soul.

Travel Tips

Reckoning

At midnight, the lights go out. I mean all of them. The house lights. The shop lights. Even the streetlights. So, without the moon, you can't see to tinkle in an unfamiliar bathroom. And... as for Baudelaire's orgy of silence I mentioned earlier? Prepare yourself. If you fear the sound of your own thoughts... if you're afraid of those thoughts you have been thinking all your life and can't stand the prospect of finally having to confront them... stay in Paris. Because, when you lie down in the bed, swaddled in the absolute dead hush of Saint

Sauvant, these thoughts will wrap their arms around your neck and begin to pet your skull. There will be no defense. And when the bells of Église Saint Sylvain mark midnight, every tab your soul has ever skipped out on will come due.

L'heuves du opévation

I cannot speak for other parts of France, but here in the region of La Charente Maritime, posted hours of business mean absolutely nothing. They stick them up in windows, or tape them to front doors, but then show up when they feel like it, and head back home whenever they damn well please. Your best bet is to arrive somewhere between about 1:00 and 3:00 p.m. and see what happens. Who knows… you might get lucky.

Give Me a Sign

To go with that, signs along the streets and highways may or may not help. It depends on what you want. If you want the name of a certain rue… good luck. If you seek direction to some beautiful village that someone told you not to miss… you might or might not see a sign for it, but more often you will see two signs for it at the same intersection, and they'll point in opposite directions. However, if you want to purchase, then drink, some Pineau or Cognac, or both, you will see a sizable, easy to read sign every half kilometer or so on every road between every town.

No Différence

Mosquitoes and flies may have prettier names in French: "moustiques" and "mouches," but their pestilential effect is the same as Texas or anywhere else.

I slapped a mosquito on our picnic by the creek today that was so big, I could have sworn I saw a beret on its head and a tiny goatee on its chin before I flattened it.

Santé

If you pride yourself on your perfect attendance record at Sunday School and your lifelong success with unfailing temperance, find another country to visit. Because in France, the rosé starts around 4:00 p.m., the chardonnay about 6:00, and the pinot noir at, say, 8:00 to 9:00 and goes to midnight. At least. N'est-ce pas?

A Bad Import

The TABAC owner does not know a word of English. But he whistled every note of Billy Joel's "You May Be Right" this afternoon when it came on the radio in the back. Music is everywhere. People whistle in their doorways. They whistle when they walk down the street. With baguettes and wine, of course.

However, if a radio is on anywhere, 9 out of 10 times it will play American pop music. And 9 out of 10 of those times it will be bad, very bad, American pop music. Not just the kind of bad that's almost sort of fun or funny in its bouncy and sing-alongy sort of badness, but the kind of bad that makes you want to learn how to apologize in French for the embarrassing truth that your homeland is responsible for this crap.

Billy Joel was a nice exception to the rule, though. And the TABAC owner seemed happy with the selection as he danced and wiped down the cappuccino machine. So, he may be right to do it.

Don't Blow It

The American tourist has one peculiar
advantage in the South of France. Here
they seem to hate Parisiens more than
Americans. We're almost "acceptable"
by comparison.

But don't get too excited about it. They
are, after all, still French. And they'll
remind you now and then, if you need.
Just be subtle and polite, roll your eyes
a little if someone speaks of Paris, and
for heaven's sake, don't walk into a cute
café on the main rue and shout,

> *Does anybody know where the heck*
> *a McDonald's or a Burger King is*
> *around here? I'm sick of all this*
> *damn moldy cheese!*

MAY THE FROMAGE
BE WITH YOU

My boy play well, and there
will be cheese. Violin. Cheese.

~ *The Red Violin*

And on the eighth day,
God said to the French:

Let there be cheese.

He went on to say:

*And let there be cheeses of all colors
and kinds, from white to orange,
even blue and green cheeses.*

Hard cheese. Soft cheese.
From fragrant to noxious.
From holey to moldy.

And then God commanded
that these cheeses go forth
and multiply all throughout
the homeland of the Gauls,

and that mankind, living
in the land at that time,
should give names
to all the cheeses…

names that will be
veritably unpronounceable
to any living outside the land.

Say, Crottin de Chavignol…
or Neufchâtel. Or maybe
Chabichou du Poitou.

Then, in order for the
French to be able to eat
well all the days of their lives,

God created the Fromagerie,
a wondrous little shiny store
devoted entirely to cheeses
so the people of the land
would always have
a huge selection.

And lo… the cheese
will be with you always…
even unto the end of the age.

And the Holy Éclair as Well

Apparently, as time passed, God also decided it was not good that the Fromagerie should be alone. So, he created for it a few companions. He took display cases from the side of the Fromagerie and made the Boulangerie, Pâtisserie, and Crêperie.

Whether in Paris, or any small city in France, a person need only walk forty to fifty feet in any direction away from the Fromagerie, and he or she will find freshly baked bread, fine pastries, or crêpes filled with Nutella and bananas,

or maybe soaked in Rum. Your choice.
But never both. Don't be greedy.

A favorite of mine—and one of the
deadliest, most addictive substances
known to human taste buds—is the
"Café Éclair." This is a long and thin
French donut injected with steroids—
steroids disguised as a coffee-flavored
crème—and then covered in a mocha
icing guaranteed to diabetically blur
your vision for a good fifteen to twenty
minutes. At only five to six inches long
and an inch in diameter, this little pastry
packs quite a caloric punch. It should
be respected, like a jalapeño in South
Texas. It should be eaten slowly, and
with a deep, lascivious joy.

And stepping on the scales, to assess
the damage, should be avoided for
weeks to come.

INVESTING IN THE MARKET

It goes without saying: It's about the food here. (It also goes without saying, by the way, that any time a person tells you that something goes without saying, it goes without saying that he's gonna go ahead and say it anyway.) But, let's get back to the food.

If you've got a bungalow in a cute village that follows the rise and fall of its hills in southern France, you must stock it with the good stuff and plan on having some meals in the European glow of some European candles, no?

The problem comes, at least in the early days of the trip, with that first venture to the supermarket where every aisle, package, and label are clearly marked, but, in a language you know little to nothing about. Certainly, many items can be taken on sight. Potatoes, onions, and carrots all look similar, only fresher and sexier over here for some reason. But, if you're wanting to know the fat content of the milk, you've got to hope that the prefix "demi-" means what you think it means in this instance. And when it comes to the coffee aisle, you won't know if it's in bean form, instant or ground, espresso or drip. And, you will have a hundred colorful options to help drive you straight to distraction.

Then, when it comes time to pay, and the bored teenager at the register quips out the total, you'll stare at all the weird looking coins in your palm and wish you'd studied the numbers in that *Idiot's*

Guide a little harder during that nine-hour flight.

Within a few days though, if you're the lucky type, some kind person in the village who speaks a little English will tell you when and where the best local market happens to be in the larger town down the road. And when you find it, as we found the Marché St. Pierre on a crisp Saturday morning, you'll begin the mental machinations of trying to decide whether you really want to go back to the States, hoping that somehow your daughter and friends will understand.

We squealed and tugged on each other's arms like fourth graders at the zoo as we walked through stands of farm-fresh, locally-grown veggies, fruits and flowers, honey and soaps. We also noticed things like quilts and, well, bicycle repair. That one cocked our heads a bit when we saw customers lined up. He must be very good.

Further on, we passed bell peppers the size of footballs, seas of stuffed and marinated olives, and white asparagus that could double as billy clubs.

On inside, we smelled row after row of hand-wrapped gourmet cheeses, artisan breads, and jams. And when I asked for some butter, the guy cut a slab of it from a bucket-sized mound of the yellowy goodness and wrapped it up in wax paper.

Ashley struggled in the "living creatures" section. The Blue Crabs, piled up in icy bins, were still moving. The fish were quite shiny, red, black, and whole with glistening sad eyes. But the chickens with heads still on, and

what I can only describe as some kind
of small rodent, actually made her neck
and shoulders twitch a bit. She clung to
me as if we were watching *The Exorcist*
in a dark theater.

We bumped into Florence Audinet, the
kind person who'd told us about this
market, there in the freak show section.
We recomposed ourselves and made
sure she saw only our awe and culinary
excitement over the entire scene, telling
her we had nothing whatsoever to rival
it back home… a thing she did not
doubt, with a flourish of her hand and
the raise of an eyebrow.

Whether at the large, Walmartish
supermarché, or over at the St. Pierre
extravaganza, one thing became clear:

the French take food—its taste, its origin, its preparation, celebration, and ingestion—very seriously.

Hell, they can't even leave something as basic and All-American as Pork & Beans well enough alone. They've gotta use lentils instead of beans, some kind of gourmet-lookin' sausage, as opposed to a good ol' tastless weiner chopped up into pieces, and then add in carrots, onions, and a little parsley as a final insult to our tradition of blandness and lack of nutritional imagination.

They even go as far as to give it a sassy name like:

SAUCISSES
DE TOULOUSE
aux Lentilles Cuisinées

LA RUE TO PARADISE

Over the days, two neighbors opened
up as living stories like flowers made of
sound and smiles—even though we
understood few words out of their
mouths.

The oldest one lived just beyond a
mysterious gate that stood decaying
between high stone walls set in the back
corner of our courtyard. The best we
could gather from other folks is that his
name was something like "Nou-nou,"
and that he'd lived in the village all his
life. Well into his 80s now, he would
pop open the gate in the mornings with
a cane and scrape his way across the

gravel to those large French doors off the kitchen that we loved to keep wide open every minute we spent in the house—a thing he appeared to appreciate.

With a population of barely 500, Saint Sauvant seems like a low-crime area, outside of the occasional drunken teenager backing into somebody's garden wall with a tractor. So, even though the open doors served as a magnet for those mosquitoes and flies I talked about earlier, as well as Nou-nou, we couldn't help but celebrate the cool air of perfect late-spring days.

With the help of bilingual dictionaries, the *Idiot's Guide*, and Ashley's four years of French in high school, we figured out he had just lost his wife of fifty to sixty years this last Christmas, but that he had children and grandchildren in the area and had just celebrated the birthday of a granddaughter. He seemed lonely, yet, somehow, in a pleasant and spunky sort of way. And when we saw him interact with other villagers at the TABAC, their faces and laughter made it clear he was also quite a character, if not a prankster and problem child, who definitely liked the "ladies."

By the time we had to pack up and leave, I was heartbroken I hadn't gotten Charles, the Audinets' son, down from the hotel to translate for a while. I could tell Nou-nou was a walking Wikipedia of stories, and I wanted to chew on a few. Alex, the local overseer of our house, told me she'd heard him speak before of hearing the thumping boots of Hitler's soldiers back in the 40s, but that he and his clan had been passed by because Saint Sauvant was too small to bother with.

Anyway, Nou-nou had been patient with us and worked with us on our French, albeit with expressive and sometimes dangerous waves of his cane. And Ashley was sad to be leaving him to all the other ladies in town. As I'm sure he was sad to see her leave. (Not so much me.)

The other neighbor of note turned out to be the first friend we'd made—the one who frightened us, just a tad, while trying to show us the ancient bread oven on our first evening in the village. He was always about, on foot, or in an old beat-up Renault—or... was it a Peugeot—and had hair as white as Nou-nou's, but seemed much younger in the bounce and spring of his gait.

Half way through the week, I'd given two of my books and a copy of my *Driftin' Away* CD to the Audinets at the hotel as a gift for all the wi-fi, Cognac, and kindness they'd offered us. This caused a minor stir I guess, as the next day Charles mentioned my website and something about my search for the perfect margarita. And later, down at the TABAC, Bertrand—our newer new friend's name—became very animated about my music. The Audinets had played him some of it, and he appeared to like it more than a little—especially after a couple of glasses of rosé, which I think happened more than once a day. I know it happened that night, since he invited us over to his house to share in a couple more rounds of a couple of glasses with him.

Bertrand lives just down from the church at the end of Rue du Paradis. And since Charles had popped over from the hotel to help translate—and to ask us about Austin, Texas—and to share in a small bag of marijuana that Bertrand kept in a slender vase by the fireplace—I asked Bertrand how he came to live at the end of Paradise Street. He said that when he moved to the village after a career in traveling sales, he had a choice between Rue de l'Enfer—Hell Street—up above the church, or down here at the far end of Paradise. And, since he'd had plenty of the other in his life, he decided it was time for a break.

The comment wasn't all made of joke, even though his face smiled. I could see tiny shards of pain reflected in the glass of rosé he raised in a toast he did not voice. And Ashley and I had noticed pictures of a young boy on the wall when we came in. When we gestured toward them, he only put both hands over his chest and repeated a few times "Mon Cœur" or "Me Cœur"—I can't remember which it was—My Heart.

And some stories are for later in a friendship. So, the rest of the night was talk about music, Texas and Oklahoma, disdain for Parisiens, and how Bertrand wished he could see my song lyrics translated into French... because... it's about the Words... *les Mots!*, he said with a finger pointing somewhere above my head before he put both hands to his chest again.

The night wore on, maybe an hour or so too long. Ashley was a trooper, though, and even went upstairs at one point to play Bertrand some James McMurtry tunes on YouTube. And he flipped for them. So things dragged on a bit longer, since he had to hear just one more McMurtry song. Or two. But, no one complained about the small new world that had big-banged in the dark space between us during these warm, unrepeatable hours. A memory I knew would live on, indefinitely.

Later, back at our place, lying in the pitch black around the bed, I got to thinking about Nou-nou and Bertrand and the quiet sorrows of people who work to stay happy in spite of life's tidal waves and tornados. I guess it surprised me how similar the pangs of loss and sorrow sound down inside the difficult vowels of French... how, when hearts break, they cry and sing, without the slightest accent, in a strange but universal tongue.

A Certain *Je Ne Sais Quoi*
(Only, Not the Good Kind)

Cognac left us a little dry.

I mean the town. Not the drink. As a drink, it may be one of our new favorite things… to the point that we might have to make room for it in that song from *The Sound of Music.*

I likely put too much trust in my weird sense of geographical intuition. I don't think I've always had it. And yet, I couldn't tell you when it developed either. But "places" sing to me. They hum inaudible tunes that vibrate the organ of a big ear that floats around in the hollows of my body. And I'm sure it's mostly in my head—the hollowness, I mean. But it's a strong sense, and these strains of harmony versus dissonance are arrestingly loud, considering they make no sound.

Anyway, back to the town. I don't know how to convey the sad grayness that hung in the humid air of Cognac—other than to say it had a sort of gray sadness to it. The streets were, I guess, superficially clean, but if you looked closer, there was a sticky film—a grime laid down from centuries of plodding soles that is never going to come up. Now that I think about it though, this applies to Paris, Amsterdam, and other European cities I've seen as well. So, it must have been something else... or more. Or less.

Maybe it had something to do with the parking receipt that I had to plug a meter box for, wait for it to print, and then place on my dashboard that made me feel oddly, if not exactly, like I was in downtown Dallas or Chicago. And neither paying for it in euros nor the phrase "FIN DE STATIONNEMENT AUTORISE," printed at the top, made the activity seem any sexier.

Maybe it was the vendor I saw on the sidewalk in the pedestrian district selling blue, green, red, and pink plastic bongs next to trays of incense on a 4 X 8 folding table that looked borrowed from the basement closet of a nearby church—that, and all of the black leather S & M lingerie he had displayed on headless white mannequins leaning against the van behind him. Or maybe it was how all the restaurants stopped serving food after three o'clock, and so—since we'd decided to take a look inside the Hennessy cognac distillery first and, of course, sample a grade or three of it—our blood sugar went haywire until we made it back to the bungalow.

Whatever it was, or wasn't, the town of Cognac did not sing to me. I know we need to give it another chance someday. And Ashley did buy the cutest little red dress from a shop on a side street. Oh, and there was this awesome boutique chocolaterie right next to it? Geez... But, still, it is just *work* for me, every time, to remember to put the "g" in front of the damn "n" when I go to spell Cognac.

RÌCORÉ - A QUICK FIX

Considering the depressed value of the
American dollar and culture against that
of the Euro and the French, I knew I'd
need a few supplies for writing at the
house. Can't just buy café crèmes all day
at the TABAC, or some inviting sidewalk
café over in Saintes. Every artistic
discipline—except maybe that of
mediocre Hollywood star, or worse,
screenwriter—requires a savage degree
of fiscal discipline. And that is the why
and the how of my introduction to the
strange dark substance that sustained
my work through our idyllic days in the
bungalow.

My best guess—as I squatted down in the coffee section near the end of the aisle at the InterMarché and squinted at the yellow and brown box—is that I would be buying 25 individual packets of instant Chickory coffee with some magnesium thrown in. It read:

Chicorée Café Solubles et Magnésium

A bachelor's degree in linguistics kind of helped me figure that one out. But the smaller print at the bottom of the package tried my confidence a bit more:

À Consommer de Préférence Avant Fin

and the other words that followed it, gave me the slight impression that the consumer might hope for an early end? Or something? But I felt sure I was wrong and bought it anyway.

Back at the house, I fired up the magically quick plug-in water-boiler-

thingy that Europeans are so fond of—
and that the Brits might die without,
when it comes to tea time—and rinsed
out a big blue mug. I dried it, poured in
the black-brown powder from a packet,
and then waited for the screaming pot
to stop its racket. Not knowing how
much water to add (a detail lost in the
translation of centilitres into any kind of
sense) I poured and stirred until the
color looked right.

Now… I've heard that some folks just
sort of "snap" on their very first
encounter with heroine. Or, is it
cocaine? I can't remember. One shot,
and they're addicts. Rìcoré was not that
good. But I could tell we were going to
be friends. By the end of the week, I
was shootin' up two to three times a
day… even adding in a little cognac
now and then, when Ashley wasn't
looking…

like I just done.

Tour de Villes

Monsieur Audinet, over cocktails at
l'hotel, recommended a couple of small
town tours we should make while here.
One had to do with two villages on
either side of La Charente River that
were downstream from Saintes. And
the other took us to the coast of the
Atlantic along the Bay of Biscay.

Taillebourg

Taillebourg, on the river, was pastoral
and quiet, very taupe and dried blood
red in color—and very closed for
business on Sunday. We climbed a
silent alley to the rocky hilltop that
hosts the Château de Taillebourg, a
castle from the Medieval Age that saw,
among others, the Hundred Years' War.
Destroyed and rebuilt more than once
during dark times of unending conflict,
it looked today quite tired and happy to
be resting, for a change, by the river.

If people were out and about in this
town, they were down on the river
picnicking, boating, or both. I would
say they looked to be "on holiday." But
in France I've learned that this might
simply mean it's a weekend, or maybe a
random Thursday.

I had asked Monsieur Audinet about
this certain quality, from behind the lip

of a small snifter filled with a terribly reasonable amount of expensive cognac, just the other night. He had joked: "Ahw… the French don't work. We sleep."

On the same occasion, I'd inquired about the name of the street where his Design Hotel sits there in Saint Sauvant, the Rue de la Raison—"the Street of Reason." (Even though the literature and website will tell you the hotel's address is 1, Rue des Francs Garçons. But I'm telling you, the blue and green street sign directly across from the front door reads: Rue de la Raison.) So, I asked him, "Is it true?"

"Of course!" he shot back, with a deep accent and growl rumbling in the "r." "Of course!" He repeated with a wry smile. And then he left me to ponder any possible implications, as well as the two addresses, on my own.

Port d' Envaux

We crossed the river below Taillebourg
and followed the signs, with a healthy
distrust, to Port d' Envaux. This time
they worked. And this time the town,
roughly the same size as Taillebourg,
bustled with activity and a Gallic sort of
excitement. Meaning reserved and well
controlled. By the laws of evolution,
thousands of years of war, brutal kings,
and guillotines seemed to become a part
of the genetic code in a people who've
borne their way through such things for
so long.

The main rue was closed to vehicles
because the "Brocante" was on. My
best guess at describing this would be:
village-wide garage sale. Tables, crates,

and sandwich boards covered in trinkets, clothes, paperbacks, and dilapidated DVDs lined the street on both sides. So, when I pulled up to the three sawhorses blocking the lanes, I knew I was in trouble. Only minor trouble though, since I was beginning to learn some things about my rental car and driving over here.

First, I had now come to terms with the reverse gear in my manual transmission Renault Megane Dci 1.5. I rolled my window down, so as not to hit my head on it during maneuvers. I then grabbed the stick with both hands, pushed in the clutch, and gave a full upper-body jerk toward me until it snapped in. No problem.

Second, the writer, and therefore lover of metaphor, in me could not leave alone the signs that redirected us on every other leg of our day trips— DÉVIATION. After all, the French did give us the wonderful literary term for *double entendre*. And I would feel so devious, being the deviant that I am, every time I would deviate from our route… to the point that Ashley ceased to be entertained by it.

Third, I discovered my way to make millions. Create a 3-D video game called *Driving and Parking in France*. It would need a snappier, more violent, title, but you get the idea. I'd program a vivid rearview mirror screen-within-the-screen effect up at the top that would show black BMWs riding your ass to within three inches of your bumper at 110 kph. And, to keep it interesting, I'd narrow the roads to one lane every couple of miles or so with oncoming traffic, often trucks, always appearing at the worst possible section of it, while the BMW is still riding your American ass. The roundabout element would really get the adrenaline pumping as you try to read signs, sometimes five or six stacked on top of each other on a single pole, while driving 60 to 70 kph in a tight circle around a tiny island of bright red, yellow, and purple flowers. Then, the final test—that only the veteran gamers would be able to pass— would have to be parking. To increase the difficulty level, I'd set this vignette in Paris. You'd have to parallel park on Boulevard St. Germain, or the Rue de Rivoli in the vicinity of the Louvre, with a taxi right behind you and honking, with only a few inches to spare in front and in back. And to make it even more realistic, I'd make the car in front of you one of those dwarfish Daimler Smart cars parked sideways with its back wheels up on the curb and its beady little headlights pointing out at the traffic whizzing by. I mean millions. I could retire. Anyway, I was talking about Port d' Envaux…

In the faces of the vendors behind each table, or in the open sliding doorways

of white vans, I saw my kin… my aunts
and cousins from southwest Oklahoma,
regular folks cleaning out closets and
attics for the same reason we all do it—
to make a few extra bucks. Someone
had Bob Dylan blazing out of a second
story window, just above the hubbub,
and was playing along on an acoustic
guitar. Of course, my cousins would've
had Toby Keith crankin' instead. Not
none o' that hippie shit. But still, I saw
it… I felt it.

And I'm afraid I saw the American
Southwest in another way as well. In the
center of town, we took a seat outside
on the terrasse of Bistrot des Halles,
and, after about twenty minutes a waiter
came to take our order for Ashley's
glass of white and my cider. After
another twenty, a different waiter
brought them out. And in these forty
minutes—combined with the next
twenty we would have to wait to order

food—we had some time to look around. So we did.

Being from Oklahoma, nothing struck me as odd at first. But when Dr. Oz drives it home day after day—by way of your sweet young wife who is trying to keep the two of you healthy—even a dolt like myself hears the message that the European diet is much healthier than ours. That's why I quickly became intrigued by the number of huge guts walking by us as they shopped the brocante. And not just a few. And not just small bulges over the belt from all that rosé and cognac. I mean full on obesity. I mean shirts that were once tucked in but simply could not hold on anymore, for the pressure.

We wondered… why Port d' Envaux? We hadn't seen it in Paris, or even in Saint Sauvant. Bertrand, Monsieur Audinet, and the TABAC owner were as thin as any men their ages needed to be.

They made me self-conscious. We spoke in whispers as to possible causes. Maybe the men of this village struck oil in their fields years ago and now just sit around all day eating croissant after croissant with beer instead of wine. Maybe the water from their wells contains high levels of partially-hydrogenated soybean oil and refined sugar. More likely though, I decided we had discovered *the town* where the McDonald's Corporation dumps the effluent from all its burger and nugget mills around the world. Yeah… that's gotta be it.

Talmont-sur-Gironde

We rate Talmont as one of our favorite near-death-by-French-road-signs experiences. On the way, one town would post a pointy sign as we entered. We would make the turn. Then, at the next roundabout with four different exits besides the one for the road we'd come in on?—Nothing. We would make a full circle, go back into the town, find a new sign pointing in a different direction than the first, then repeat steps two through four. One intersection a few miles outside of Saugon blessed us with two signs to Talmont that shot off two options at a perfect 90° angle from each other. *Fantastique!*

Yet, after much gnashing of teeth, and shoulder-wrenching reversal of car, we did find our way to one of our favorite villages of the trip.

Talmont-sur-Gironde is a miniature Carmel, California packed into every square inch of a rounded and very steep outcropping on top of a cliff that overlooks the Bay of Biscay. Best I could tell, we had stumbled onto a sardine-can of a commune for wealthy and/or successful artists, with maybe a few of the "just wealthy who like to live close to artists" thrown in.

I judged this by the careful analyzation of a few observations. The first came from a quick overview of prices on a menu behind glass in front of a nice, very blue restaurant. The next had to do with a practice I have plied for many years because my mother is an excellent impressionistic painter—I did some drive-by critiquing of the art for sale in the shops and mini galleries. I don't want to say Thom Kinkade here, but it was the type of art wealthy people buy because they're visiting and can afford a hell of a lot more than a post card. And last, I've read enough biographies to begin honing the sense that truly great, thoughtful, probing, and innovative—and therefore unpopular—artists have never been able to afford living in these places. I could be wrong about all this, though. And, none of it is the point.

We had a delightful time wandering the gravel paths and lanes overgrown with hollyhocks. We took photos. We took a little bread and wine we'd slipped into a backpack. We held hands, looked out over the bay, contemplated the hilltop cemetery, the honeybees, and eventually sat down to a tasty little lunch at La Talmontaise on the quiet, uninhabited terrasse. Ashley got a French version of a caprese salad. And I ordered their house crêpe—a culinary montage involving ham, melted white cheese, and a sunny side up fried egg with the round edges of the crêpe folded up and over in four places to make the egg look like it was wrapped in a puffy gift box. Absolutely sensual when washed down with a pale cider.

For balance, I should mention a couple of things that make the Carmel-by-the-Sea comparison a poor one. First, the water in the Bay of Biscay reflected the same tones and hues as the streets of Paris's Latin Quarter the morning after a long night of public debauchery. No romantic poet wants to invoke taupe as a color of the ocean. Besides, outside of the overused word "hope," what on earth would rhyme with it?

I gaze now upon the muddy muck
of these waters, so gray and taupe…

The other thing might be that the shoreline is mostly razor-edged rock that lines a vertiginous drop-off. And, in the few spots where there is sand? It looks like it would slice your feet up just as effectively. (Of course, Carmel has its downsides as well. But it's been a few years since I walked along its feather-soft golden shores at sunset. So I can't remember any.)

The punctuation on this experience came toward the end of our lunch. A bright yellow helicopter, with even brighter red stripes, blasted out from behind a blanket of trees and then panned in a slow tight circle around us. The big side door to the metal hornet was wide open, and I soon made out that a large video camera on a mount with a goggle-eyed technician behind it was trained straight on us. For just the briefest second, I thought, "Wow! My most recent book must be doing better than I expected." But, it only took the next second for the reality to return to me that poets have never had to worry about the paparazzi. Just the king's guillotine.

So, if they were filming a commercial for this quaint village, I'm afraid that might be a last straw for its relative peace and quiet. And a tall gift shop attendant we encountered on the jaunt back to the car soon confirmed that the place absolutely teems with tourists in mid to late summers. He held a glass of rosé and a cigarette, both in his left hand, while he fiddled with a box of doodads over by the open front door— a skill we both admired. He had long black hair that fell in ratty waves, and he seemed to feel the same way we did about hordes. But, he also let us know that if we ever did make the mistake of coming back over during those summer months, we should make our way here on a Tuesday night. All the shops, cafés, and galleries stay open until midnight. But they shut the electricity off around sunset. So the whole village is lit only by the glow of hundreds and hundreds of candles. The sight of it alone might be worth the exaction of a summer horde. And we assured him, if we ever did make the mistake, we wouldn't miss it.

A Dark and Good Silence

> I asked him for news of God, and
> whether he had seen him recently.
> He replied with an indifference
> tinged with sadness: "We bow to
> each other when we meet like two
> well-bred old gentlemen, whose
> innate courtesy is, nevertheless,
> not sufficient to wipe out the
> memory of old grudges."
>
> ~ Baudelaire
> "The Generous Gambler"
> *Paris Spleen*

Every day, we walked up to it, then
turned to duck into the hotel instead for

an apéritif or dinner, or both. But I eyed the solidity and silence of the Eglise Saint Sylvain every time it came into view. And in a village this size, that means… everywhere you turn. I could see the slate gray tower from our bathroom window. It loomed around the last corner on my short walks to the TABAC, and on every curve of our daily drives back into the house from the main road. But it took all week to finally drag ourselves up and into the building.

The heavy wooden door sang of its war-torn and prayer-filled years as it swung open. Once inside, a few high windows and the sun through the open doorway gave the only light we had to go on. The floors and walls shivered and shrank back from the blast of light. And they radiated the sense that they may well have given rise to the term *stone cold*.

The gray below bled up into a motley white of vaulted ceilings. Where the three naves met, a scant number of wooden chairs and pews sat scattered about as if they had all been caught playing cards in the absence of much business as of late. They exhibited little to no remorse though, since they'd been playing under the immediate gaze of Christ, still crucified, on a large cross hanging on the inside front corner of the right-hand nave. I now felt as though I were the guilty party for the intrusion.

For a Southern Baptist boy who's always visited Catholic missions and cathedrals because Baptists—in their fear of art—have left behind little architecture of historical interest, the first thing that struck me was the overall lack of ornateness. Sure, the altar that crowned the semicircular wall at the head of the apse flashed its six green and white marble columns with gold-leafed capitals—a striking and very tall assemblage with a cross on top. It definitely showed a pilgrim which way to face. But the structure itself shows what happens when monks are left in charge of building campaigns (as opposed to wealthy merchants in Rome.) Monks have most often made better brewmeisters than they have architects and interior decorators. And I would just as soon they stay that way.

But as I stood there, smug inside my clever idea of inanimate objects playing poker, and my critique of Romanesque architecture, for which I hold no credentials, I turned to look at the nails in the feet of Christ. The crucifix may not have been life-sized, but it seems like it was in retrospect. And there they were, maybe a meter above my head… the two feet… the two nails… and two glazed drops of blood just beneath the head of each nail.

Lightning struck behind my eye sockets. And after the thunder trailed off, the musty silence of the hall wrapped around my throat. My body quaked. But the stone beneath my shoes held firm. I found a bench against the back wall of the nave and sat down, shivering in the wake of an aftershock.

Mon Dieu. What the hell? I may have said out loud.

I began to weep. I put my hands to my face like I was stuffing rags into a bad door seal during a hurricane. But it was too late. Something had snapped in my infrastructure—maybe from bad design, but more likely from the wear and tear of the last twenty years.

What is wrong with me? I did ask out loud. But, of course, I had a rough idea. I have experienced the same kind of spiritual deluge at Chimayó in New Mexico and the Church of Saint Anne in Jerusalem. Something about the pure and exquisite absence of any and all followers of Christ in a space like this reminds me of the things I loved about Jesus… about belief… about good stories… about having some answers for at least some questions when I was younger. What have I got now? A hostile, entropic universe and a truck-load of well-educated cynicism, both accompanied by an increase in the early symptoms of arthritis. Seems I could've done better.

"Well then, come back," cry the ghosts of the righteous, the singers of banal praise songs, and the teetotalers of perfect Sunday School attendance. There are so many. Hundreds. And not one realizes that a good number of them were the reason I left. But I can't see how any of it matters now. That water is long under the bridge and well out to sea by now. To this day, my parents, and a very few others, remain the only examples I see of what it might mean to be a good Christian. And as for the leadership in the Southern Baptist Convention, for decades now, I see them as little more than theological criminals and cutthroats. —*Adieux Messieurs!*—, I growl every time I think of them and their ilk.

As for these occasional breakdowns? I welcome them. It feels good, cleansing, and comforting to stand in the warm presence of something higher—a better idea, misinterpreted as I believe it to be. And, it does feel cathartic to cry for a while… just to soak in the sorrow of those little drops of blood above his toes, and to feel… down to the depths of my entrails… that the Lord of All Creation would not appreciate more all the praise songs in the world than he likely does my silence and these tears.

There Will the Cheese Be Also

That last day you spend in any paradise is always a cocktail of feelings. The sour of having to leave mingles with the sweet things of home—Cayenne's furry face and brown eyes, so ready for a walk, and that good familiar bed. And the more I travel, the more I love my bathroom. You know what I'm talking about. You're just too polite to mention it. So, with all of that sweet and sour mingling in the shaker, we wanted to make sure we added some kick to it— the most important ingredient in every cocktail.

We began with a bottle of champagne in a soft patch of grass some little ways down and off from the gravel road that runs by the house. We'd brought a blanket, two glasses, and two market-fresh strawberries—one for each glass. We'd packed two big chunks of orange cheese as well. But, by now I assume you take for granted that wherever there is alcohol, there will the cheese be also. As will the sundried-tomato-stuffed olives and artichoke hearts.

We sprawled out there, next to what appeared to be the headwater of a fresh underground spring. And in the halo of an absolute void of traffic noise, along with a few of those French flies and mosquitoes, we engaged in the rather anachronistic activity of "just talking." We talked for a long time too. No cell phones, no earbuds, no loud car stereo nearby, burning up the battery. We just talked. And long enough to polish off an entire bottle of bubbly.

To all the teens and 20-somethings who might roll eyes at the archaic ideas and pastimes of those who are a lot less older than you think, go ahead and roll those healthy young irises. It matters not to me that you have no experience with just how sexy and luscious a face to face conversation with a "real" friend can be. Or how much a breeze through the cottonwoods dancing on the soft silence of slow-moving water adds to it. We bow before your superior ways and knowledge. And do, please, continue on with your screens. It just means more soft patches of grass for us.

Later in the afternoon I held court on the patio of the TABAC for one last writing session. It was my second time in one day, and when I ordered that

damn *bueno* candy bar again—because
there's nothing else to munch on but
huge croissants and colored marshmallows—the owner patted his belly
with both hands and said, *Gourmand!*,
through the squinted teeth of a gotcha
grin. The meaning he intended will not
be what you find in the dictionary. But I
understood well enough and returned a
half-hearted smile with a shoulder shrug
of culpability. I will miss so much all the
café crèmes and the general linguistic
confusion of this little place—a sweet
confusion that guarantees I'll be left
thoroughly alone when I write.

For our last supper, we'd decided days
ago to go out in style with a fine meal at
the Design Hotel. We began with an
apéritif, a cognac and Schwepps, which

the Audinets had taught us was what one simply must do before a meal. This we shared down a few steps from the dining room in their stylish and trés petite bar—a space that gives you the feeling you're hanging out in the front room of Madonna's Upper East Side townhouse, while waiting on a few insanely well-dressed people to go out for a drink at some hot watering hole that you'll ill be able to afford. Except, more relaxed than that.

The dining room hosts only six tables. Silver bases with glass tops, standing on white tile. White chairs with red backs. Red water glasses with a carafe covered in silver chain mail. (You may recall some previous excitement about that.) And, in honor of that color scheme, Ashley began with a glass of white wine, and I with a glass of red. We toasted a beautiful end to a beautiful honeymoon in the ridiculously beautiful Southwest of France, and then spent some time looking over the white pages in our red menus.

To be in a hurry, when dining in this land, defies one of many among a subtle set of irrefutable laws and rules about food and drink. By now, we had leaned back into this mode of culinary being. So, if it took twenty minutes for an appetizer of five small prawns to show up, there was always the wine and the glowing eyes of a loved one—and, therefore, very little to worry about, when you get down to the roots and truffles of it all.

Ashley's white fish and my red steak maintained the evening's color scheme. And, while both were delicious, they were, merely, a means to dessert. And what else would dessert in France be?

Cheese, of course.

BIENVENUE
(BACK TO PARIS, BABY)

The A10 highway, and the tollbooth at the Bordeaux end of it, went smoothly enough, on our way back to the train station. I almost felt cocky—the kind of cocky that fools you into thinking you could return someday and do the whole thing all over again without a hitch. It's the same feeling that grips you on a rare afternoon of golf, when your dreaded 5-iron connects so perfectly with that Titleist 1 and it sails 170 yards to the green. You begin to believe it 'could' happen again—much like a poor soul in Las Vegas believes he can turn that fifty bucks he just won into a hundred.

We even experienced a small sense of mastery over the train ride this time around. We each took one half of a Dramamine tablet to fight off those roly polies playing footsies inside our stomachs. It allowed me to write, and it completely knocked out poor Ashley. I actually worried about her there for a while, but she stirred and came around as we neared Paris.

When the stewardess rolled by with the snack cart I ordered a café with a little crème on the side. And, since Ashley wasn't watching, I added on a bar of TOBLERONE. I broke off the triangular spikes of chocolate happiness one at a time and lost myself in a daydream of what it would be like to grow up Swiss and do nothing but make fantabulous chocolate for a living. But I cut the silly reverie short. Because, most livings—no matter how exotic the locale or the product of manufacture—tend to lose their Honey-and-Almond-Nougat lining after any amount of time spent laboring in the business.

It's like the way the city of love won't necessarily care that you are on your honeymoon, so it makes you stand— with everyone else—in a lengthy line waiting for a taxi on the dingy curb of an exhaust-clouded catacomb beneath the Gare Montparnasse. The moment was enhanced by an older woman who looked a lot like Queen Elizabeth on a reduced income, and none too happy about it to boot, as she stood in the line in front of us griping about the wait in French. We smiled and nodded our approval of her disapproval, until a black cab finally swallowed her frown. I'd say it took twenty to thirty minutes for her to get hers, and at least another five to ten for ours.

When we finally jerked and jetted out into the madness of the traffic on Boulevard de Vaugirard, I noticed that the meter on the dashboard of the taxi was already at 2.30 €. But, as I opened my mouth to call him on it, I whispered to myself instead:

Hey, it's Paris baby…

…gotta payer to jouer.

I'm sure the French
have done many things of import
but
it smells of the past.

to go to Paris to create art
now
would be much like sitting around
waiting for a butterfly to fart.

~ Charles Bukowski
"just another bad affair"
Dangling in the Tournefortia

A Shower and a Bed

Only
the loving
madness that
overtakes otherwise
reasonable minds when on
their honeymoon, would sweet-talk
two poor teachers into a 400-dollar
hotel room for one night—especially
when it's a room in which they will
spend very little time… because…
they're in Paris, for heaven's sake!

There is much food to eat, much more
wine to drink, the taxi leaves for the
airport at 7:00 a.m., and it is already
midafternoon. We will, at most, shower

off the train ride in a bit of a rush, hit the town for all we've got, and then—if all goes responsibly—sleep maybe five hours, tops, before the wakeup call.

That said, the Hotel Regina looked magnificent when the driver performed a few ballet-like traffic violations and whipped us up in front of it on the Place des Pyramides. As it sits across the Rue de Rivoli from the Musée des Arts Décoratifs, and catty-cornered to the Jardin des Tuileries, I was shocked by the good location. We were walking distance to everything you want to do and see if you've only got sixteen hours and don't care to see the Eiffel Tower.

An attendant in a dark navy-blue suit whisked away our luggage before I had a chance to develop any sense of trust in his character. So, as I watched him disappear with it through a massive wooden door at the far end from the main entrance, I paid off the taxi driver and let the 2.30 overcharge go. I just considered it a luxury tax—a fee for the luxury of still being alive after that maniacal ride.

Once inside the famous revolving door, my adjectives shifted from "impressive" to words like "stately" and "regal." Built to open on the occasion of the first World's Fair in 1900, I could almost taste the funk of a hundred years in the solid oak and glass of its Art Nouveau design. And, yes, I looked that up. I do not have an encompassing knowledge of four and five star hotels around the world stored in my mind. We all google now and then. Besides, I would rather live life than be a walking and talking encyclopedia. I mean, we've got the omniscient Wiki-thingy ever at our fingertips.

The elevator is stately and regal too, and old enough to make a body nervous. But our room, though small—like

European bathrooms—is, simply, opulent. We've got a long balcony that is a reasonably-sized person's width. To the left, the Louvre. To the right, the Jardin des Tuileries. And beyond that, the Eiffel Tower... about as close as it needs to be.

After I took the nine to twelve or so pillows off the bed to lie down while Ashley showered, I could not believe my view of that tower. It gave me a chance to revel in the forty-plus dollars we were saving by not riding up to the top—about the price of a margarita at Bar Hemingway. Not that I was thinking about it.

WHAT MONEY CAN'T BUY

Apparently, no amount of money—not even $400 for a small hotel room for one night—can buy a functional shower in France. Both hotels in Paris provided us with only a detachable sprinkler head at the end of a short stainless steel rope in a small bathtub that had a foot-wide and maybe four-foot-tall pane of glass that I guess was to serve as a splash-guard for the sink, in case someone else wants to brush her teeth while you're wrestling the water cobra—which of course would depend on whether or not the two of you are small enough people to be *in* a French bathroom at the same time. (See "Reveries")

The problem is one of physics. Multiple streams of water shooting out from a mobile apparatus that is wielded by the nondominant hand of a human male just has trouble written all over the steamy white tiles of the tight walls. It sprayed the ceiling, the bath mat, and the bidet. I made enough racket that Ashley knocked and asked if I was okay in there. At one point I fumbled the ball and a plume or two made it all the way over to the toilet, even managing to get our one roll of toilet paper damp.

This brings me to two other things that the inflated euro can't buy: towels and toilet paper. To say that the towels are threadbare and rough only gets you part of the way to what I want you to feel. Now, try to imagine those 20-year-old scraps that you keep under bathroom sink for when the dog throws up or the commode overflows. Yeah... there you go. The housekeeping staff does find a way to keep them surprisingly white, somehow, but outside of that…

French toilet paper is, at least, not of the Russian sandpaper variety. That's the good news. The not so good news is that it still plies its trade with roughly the consistency and texture of a no-name low-grade paper towel from the Dollar General. Are you with me now? Can you close your eyes and really… Okay, maybe that's going too far. But I hope you get what I'm going for.

Ah, but it's Paris. And you've got to clean up somehow for that last night of your honeymoon. So, feel the burn, don your best duds, and get yourself ready for that beautiful cliché of a midnight kiss on that magnificent cliché of a Paris bridge over the Seine… because, even for a recovering cynic, this whole Technicolor shebang actually *is*… about as good as it gets.

Arts du Gastronome

My friend Connie from Austin emailed a plea that we find Café Marly by the Pyramide du Louvre, and could we "please order," for her, "the panne cotta with strawberry and rosewater purée on top,"—a very specific request, and, therefore, one that stood out among the multitude of suggestions we received in the weeks before leaving. I'll add to that, though, that I like Connie quite a bit and have come to trust and respect her exquisite tastes in art and gastronomy—two things that verge on being redundant in my book. That said, for two people who adore food and drink beyond reason, deciding where to eat in Paris is like choosing which person in the overcrowded lifeboat is going to have to die in order to save the others. It causes a physical pain in our chests.

The noble stone columns that support the arcades above the terrace of the Richelieu wing immediately made me self-conscious about my black t-shirt and sad blue jeans. They appeared to make the maître d' at Café Marly self-conscious for me as well. He led us across the terrace with a courteous disdain washing over his cheeks and tightly shut mouth. As an accent, he kept his left eyebrow cocked up in a perfect pyramid above his obsidian eye. This particular affectation, though, looked like it might've been a tattoo— something made permanent. You know, to save him all the muscular trouble.

He handed us off to a hostess at the front door who was more tolerant, because she was indifferent. She did, however, seat us at a lovely little table in the back corner at the far end of the room. We chose to sit inside because the terrace required a wait, as well as a certain degree of pretention we didn't feel we could maintain for the entire meal. Besides, our corner was quiet, cool, and very black and red with a warm gold trim.

For the life of me, I don't recall our waiter ever uttering more than one, maybe two, words. He wasn't rude, just robot-like, yet graceful. Yes, there was some grace to his movements… as if he'd been programmed to gracefully meet our needs, but not to encourage us to enjoy our stay in France—nor to ever feel the need to come back.

So, it turns out he was the third human spark to help light the little revolution that was firing up its engines inside me from the moment the maître d' had looked down at my sad jeans. And that's why, after he took Ashley's polite order, something in me snapped. The waiter stepped over, and in my best Southwest American, I said, "Yeah... I'll take a mojito and the cheeseburger there," pointing at the menu where it said, simply and only, "cheeseburger" in all small case letters. I don't know what made me do it. I still shake my head when I think about it. I mean, if I'd wanted a poor man's sandwich, I at least could have ordered the Croque Monsieur, a sort of French version of a glorified ham and cheese sandwich that is blanketed in an extra outer layer of greasy white cheese. And, I am still somewhat embarrassed by the order, as was Ashley, bless her kind and sweet heart. But I maintain, and will forever, that they pushed me to it. And it embarrasses me even more to now have to report—with my smartass's hat in my compunctious hand—that the burger was... *ab-so-lument fantastique!*

Therefore, they trumped me. They got the last laugh. And when I get got, I'll be the last to admit it. But I will, at least, admit it. Our meal was appealing, pleasant, and delicious. Scrumptious rolls, and a fingerbowl of freshly whipped butter, showed up with our drinks. My mojito came with three to four stems of mint, and at least as many slices of lime muddled in it. And that's not counting the entire mint plant that was sticking out the top of it, or the thick round slice of lime that adorned the rim like a big handle. My burger arrived on white porcelain soon after, smothered in cheddar cheese. The top of the bun had been lightly toasted and laid, flipped over, to the side, and it had a perfectly round and healthy dollop of what appeared to be a chipotle mayo sauce of some kind. Lettuce, red onion, and a tomato slice sat next to the bun top. And then, next to those, was an exquisitely reasonable portion of potato chips served in a white porcelain cup.

It's as if they were saying, "We shall offer you this American dish, but with such style, and of course grace—not to mention *sans* the pound and a half of baked beans and potato salad on the side—that we shall shame you not only for having ordered it, but even unto the ends of every time you order it from this time forward at some Chili's or Fudrucker's back home, realizing, each and every time, that you Americans eat completely insane and embarrassing amounts of food." (Hard to argue with them.)

And so, I was duly humbled by the gastronomic indictment. I was utterly enamored of the splendid textures and tastes of the meal. And, there was no way I was going to be so dad-gummed American as to then pile on an order of panne cotta to the end of it. So now I even have to go home and apologize to Connie for having failed her in her simple request.

But, even after the ordeal, I must say that I would come back to this place in a heartbeat. Maybe in my blue jeans again... maybe not. But I'd order a small salad with some tea next time...

before diving into the panne cotta.

GAUCHE AND PROUD

The primary definition of the French
word "gauche" in my bilingual *Larousse
Mini Dictionary* is "left." "Gaucher"
means "left-handed." But the second
definition of "gauche" is "awkward,"
which is accompanied by a parenthetical
suggestion of a synonymous relation to
the word "maladroit"—a term that
exists in both English and French
(borrowed by the former, and yet
pronounced much more beautifully in
the latter). Both languages, though,
define it with precisely the same word:
"clumsy." My *Oxford Minireference for
English* adds to that: "bungling."

But let us return now to "gauche," which the French use interchangeably as "left" and "awkward." English then borrowed this word as well, since, for the most part, English lacks linguistic originality—except, maybe, in its extraordinary capacity to steal and then integrate. I don't, of course, intend for that to reflect or imply anything where English Literature is concerned. Unless it turns out to be a legitimate concern centuries from now, in which case I'd like to go on record for having raised the question in the early 2000s.

Anyway, the *Oxford's* definition for "gauche" in English ups the ante from the French. It claims the term means "socially awkward." Which brings me to the only thing I wanted to get at with this whole lexical mess. And that would be: as a lifetime lefty, I find every damn bit of it offensive.

SANTE!
. . . TO THE MAN

But in the story the boys were
drinking and this made me
thirsty and I ordered a rum St.
James.

~ Ernest Hemingway

This brief sentence came flying out of
A Moveable Feast as early as page five.
And since I was sitting on the plane
somewhere over the Atlantic when I
first read it, eating the airline's hard,
crusty rolls and drinking lukewarm
ginger ale because I refuse to pay ten
dollars for a mini of bad tequila, it's

understandable that I would begin to develop a plan to hunt down a rum St. James, once in Paris, and sip it down in the old man's honor.

Dreams such as these make it possible for people like me to survive nine-hour flights against the earth's rotation. And dreams such as these sustain us through the 45-minute descent and eventual landing—a process that still seems to us, no matter how many times we've done it, to be a crime against physics. But, when I tossed my bags into the room at Hotel Dauphine and set out on my quest—having now survived the landing *and* the taxi ride, which I did not realize would be even more scary and dangerous—no menu in any café had rum St. James on the list. And no bar had it behind the counter, glowing in the reflection of its big mirror. We searched for two days. Nothing. So I had to head south to Bordeaux with my sober tail between my stable and steady legs. And though this might sound like a piddly thing to some, I don't handle failure well—especially when it comes to comestible crusades. (I'm going to counseling for this, but I have a long way to go.)

Anyway, that's why, when we returned to Paris with only nine to ten hours to spare before a little sleep and the flight home, I could not contain my joy when we stumbled across Le Zinc d' Honoré only a few blocks away from the Hotel Regina. This sidewalk café drew us in because it offered some afternoon shade. And when we picked up the menu I, fortunately, did not make a sound, but grabbed my chest instead. There it was: Rhum Ambré St. James. We sat down. We waited the required twenty minutes for a waiter. He seemed sort of a nice guy, with a mild case of Tourette's. Ashley ordered champagne. I asked for the rum St. James. And we decided to split a banana and Nutella crêpe, because it's one of the many things one should do in Paris, and we had euros we didn't want to have to exchange when we got home.

The rum arrived in a tiny snifter. It was the deepest gold, verging on a burnt bronze. I swirled it in the glass, brought it up to my nose, even though you're probably not supposed to do that with rum, then raised up its bounty in a shotgun toast to the sky. And in the sweet and sad burn of that first sip, I recalled the sentence Hemingway had followed with on page five:

> This tasted wonderful on the cold day and I kept on writing, feeling very well and feeling the good Martinique rum warm me all through my body and my spirit.

Then, in walked the pretty girl at the café where he was writing, "with a face fresh as a newly minted coin," and with hair as "black as a crow's wing." But, she left, and he never saw her again. So, I took a second drink and reveled in the flush along my throat as I looked across the table at the girl who has decided to stay. She smiled a banana Nutella smile, and I thought, "You lucky bastard…" then felt, all of a sudden, overwhelmed with an intoxicating gratitude. I rested inside that for a moment and had a bite of the crêpe. Wow… it really was that good. And that's when I reached for another petite swig of the sugar cane. This one just to thank the Reverend Edmond Lefebure, Father Superior, and those good friars of the Monastery of the Brothers of Charity way down in Martinique for their extraordinary skills in alchemy… and…

for making this moment possible.

Hemingway Revisited

Paris, the town best organized for
a writer to write in that there is,

~ Hemingway

So, true to my word, I finished reading
Ernie's *Feast* by trip's end. I feel a bit
smug about it. But, now that I'm done,
do I still feel the same uncertainty about
Hemingway's writing? Yeah… to an
extent. Did I like the book anyway?
Absolutely. It's a captain's log of sorts.
It's not, however, the celebration that
the title suggests. Instead, I found it
more a commiseration for artists who

want some evidence that their miserable lives are not the only miserable lives to have graced their profession. And he somehow pulled this off while still filling us with the romantic desire to feel up Paris for ourselves.

> You belong to me and all Paris belongs to me and I belong to this notebook and this pencil.

He even comes close to reconvincing us that there might be some truth to that old truism—the truism that, as we get older, we often stop believing is true—the one that claims our poorest years are the best ones:

> But this is how Paris was in the early days when we were very poor and very happy.

What I saw as most impressive though, was the way he somehow made the darker and more negative stories hit home with a kind of subversive inspiration. It helps me to know that the author who brought us *The Great Gatsby* was insecure about the size of his penis. He was also a hypochondriac. And, Fitzgerald probably would have delivered many more great books had it not been for his certifiable wife Zelda who, along with her mental illness, was jealous of F. Scott's writing success and, therefore, worked overtime to keep him drunk and partying so he wouldn't have the energy to work. A thing that made Hemingway both sad and angry. And F. Scott simply blamed Paris. Which made Hemingway angrier. Thus the quotation I began with.

It's also interesting to find out that Gertrude Stein had pathetic fights with her lover, and yet thought that D. H. Lawrence's novels were "pathetic and preposterous." And that if someone mentioned James Joyce more than once, he never got invited back to one of her parties. And to learn that Ford

Madox Ford was rude, forgetful, obese, smelled bad, and looked like a "well clothed, upended hogshead." Or that Wyndham Lewis wore wide-brimmed black hats, had the face of a frog, and the eyes of "an unsuccessful rapist." And yet, at the same time, to hear Hemingway speak of Ezra Pound, whom I have yet to appreciate as a poet, as "always a good friend" and "always doing things for people," makes me want to read him more with an eye to reconsider, despite having died an insane racist in an asylum.

In the end, I come back to what I said in my earlier reflections: I love the one-line zingers. And so many of them helped me confirm suspicions, like:

> We still went under the system, then, that praise to the face was open disgrace.

I've always felt that way. But he put it in a short sentence. His gift. So, I feel I must recant. If you're going to Paris… especially for the first time… maybe you should still go ahead and bring along *A Moveable Feast*.

(As long as you buy this book to go with it.)

> Paris was always worth it and you received return for whatever you brought to it.

O THE INANITY

Now you could get out and hope
it was an accidental visit and that
the visitor had only come in by
chance and there was not going to
be an infestation.

~ Hemingway

Speaking of Ernest and misanthropy,
and our mutual disdain for all human
interruption, I've been ten days without
my cell phone now. We decided to set
up only one phone for international
calling and leave the other at home. So,
being the considerate new husband, I
volunteered to let Ashley take care of it.

And, now that I look back over the past week and a half, I'll tell you… I was in no way prepared for how rapturously wonderful it was going to be. I am thinking in almost Lewis Carollian terms here, with jubilant phrases like "O frabjous day!" And words like "Callooh!" and "Callay!"

To hunch down over a café crème at the Café Le Petit Cluny close to the Boulevard St. Michel, or some such place, and feel that brief sense of dis-orientation—a strange… well… sort of peace… one that I'm not used to—and then realize, Oh yeah! No phone! (As I snap fingers above my head.) What a luscious vacuum of inane disruption!

I knew it was something…

POETS, PIRATES,
AND PAINTERS

. . . and, like an amorous whisper,
the myriad music of life.

~ Baudelaire
"Already!" *Paris Spleen*

Don't bend down too close
to the ground here in Paris.

All the dust, disappointments,
and funereal unrest of its poets,
and pirates, and painters—
    alive, or dead now
    for centuries—

will begin to whisper
for you to come closer,
    then, a little closer.

There will be a secret
they want to tell you.

The People in Paris always look
busy, when all they actually do is
roam around from morning to
night...

                    ~ Céline
            Journey to the End of the Night

If you put a hand over
your eyes and stop gazing
in the window of the Louvre
or up at the Arc de Triomphe,

you'll hear Cézanne muttering,
We live in a rainbow of chaos,
or Monet's mournful lament,
My life has been nothing but a failure.

I speak of Boredom
    which with ready tears
dreams of hangings
    as it puffs its pipe.

~ Baudelaire
"To the Reader"
Les Fleurs du Mal

And the dust in the cracks
    of the Quai Voltaire,
the monumental disappointment
    of Charles Baudelaire,

even the insatiable unrest
    of a Paul Gauguin...
        or Picasso's hand...

are not trying to push you away.
They do not want you to leave.

They merely seek your permission
to step on your rose-colored glasses
and toss them into the River Seine
with a bow to common sense.

Paris is the City of Light
that harbors many darknesses.
Darknesses filled to the brim
with such insufferable beauty.

The reason so many of its songs
are sad with love, its losses,
and accordion tears.

> They came from the four corners
> of the earth, driven by hunger,
> plague, tumors, and the cold, and
> stopped here. They couldn't go
> any further because of the ocean.
> That's France, that's the French
> people.

~ Céline
Journey to the End of the Night

From Our Mistakes

I wish I could call it a whim… two young lovers listening to the laugh of love and acting on it in a flash of desire. But, I'm not young. And besides, we'd talked for days now about going back— straight in the face of sound reason— for a farewell round of drinks at Bar Hemingway.

Ashley had passed on their famous dry martini the first time—a silvery thing "served at -18.3 degrees C° in a cristal martini glass of the same temperature," according to the menu devoted entirely to cocktails. And for a martini maven, who loves her vodka with as much passion as I do my tequila, forgoing it on our previous visit was not as much a mistake on her part as it was an unpardonable sin on mine.

Along with that, the margarita situation in France had been, as I'd predicted, nonexistent since our first visit to the back alley of the Ritz. And so, as you can well imagine, I was beginning to experience symptoms of fermentation-related depression and fatigue.

Yet, the truth of it is, Ashley had those extra euros burning a hole in her purse. And, as I mentioned earlier, having to exchange them when we got back home would be a pain. So… a couple of 50-dollar drinks, we decided, it would be.

PERSPECTIVE

On the way over to Rue Cambon for
one last night of licentious spending, I
witnessed another one of those "other"
snapshots of Paris.

As we walked a main drag, I happened
to see a young white-gloved policemen
standing on a busy corner talking and
gesturing to someone, a foreign visitor
it appeared, who seemed very confused
about her current location.

The gloves looked so white, so cottony,
and so clean. I couldn't take my eyes off
of them. They waved and pointed with
an impatient kindness—a kindness that

looked like it could soon run out. But the officer's dark uniform and his hat were understated, almost invisible, in comparison. A shiny button here. A boring stripe or two there. No, it was those gloves, like two snowy doves fluttering above the filthy sidewalk. I was dazed by the brightness and heavy contrast.

And, I was enamored of the eerie way the white glove on his right hand occasionally came to rest on the very black semi-automatic .45 caliber pistol in its black holster.

38 Rue Cambon

This time, we marched straight to it—
the poor man's entrance off the alley to
Bar Hemingway, the doggy-door to the
Ritz Paris. And we stepped in without
any hesitation tonight, knowing the
worst that could happen would be that
we might get kicked out of the city. So,
bring it on.

We took a small table near the door,
since our upper room had been invaded
by meddlers. We sensed an immediate
rightness about it though. The black
wood and faded hunter green chairs
were just as comfy. We still had a photo
of "Papa" watching our backs. And this

time we told the waitress about the honeymoon thing. So, before long, we had her and the bartender both working in concert to keep us happy.

I noticed our purple friend still holding his post at the end of the bar. He looked grumpy tonight. But he had a damn good reason. Right behind him, some pretentious group of American businesspersons—five men and one woman—had taken over a large coffee table and were chatting loudly, through even louder bursts of laughter, about the weirdest people in their parts of the office building back home. One freak masturbates in the bathroom during work hours. The other guys around the table acted as if they were grossed out by the revelation and could *not* believe it. The woman was the only one who didn't seem shocked at all. Which tells us exactly what all the guys around her are doing in the bathroom during their coffee breaks.

Anyway, I agreed with our grumpy friend—who was, by the way, decked out in the same purple outfit—and I would have helped him push the whole lot of them out that doggy-door had he gone for it.

Damn Americans.

This time there was no hem hawing or nervous twitching when we surveyed the menu. We knew what we had come for, so we aimed and, when the waitress returned, we pulled the trigger. Ashley ordered her dry martini, and I went straight back for the margarita, with only one variation: I decided to go with the "Black Salt from Palm Island" on the rim. You know… to bring in a taste of the tropics. Every honeymoon needs that. But also to prove to my young bride that I am not old and set in my ways. Well, all that and because it was the longest most exotic name on the list of salts.

And we pulled that trigger right in the shadow of the shotgun mounted above the back of the bar. The sight of it gave me pause for reflection. I couldn't keep from thinking about the bar's namesake offing himself with something of the same caliber—a thought to help keep some perspective on fame, fortune, and the spooky perfection of our evening, so far.

Speaking of perspective…

Ashley interrupted my reverie with an observation that the margarita I just ordered costs more than the silver wedding band we'd bought for me on the sidewalk in Santa Fe. A sudden, yet brief, self-consciousness reached out and grabbed me by the billfold. But I soon relaxed when I realized that this is the stuff life's stories are made of. And a life without stories is not worth the dirt they put us under at the end.

So, when the drinks arrived—hers with
the wine-colored bell of a Night Cap
calla lily poking out the top, and mine
with the jet-black salt around the rim—
we raised them in a toast…

    to cheap wedding rings
    and expensive cocktails

    to fiscal irresponsibility,
    when it's sure to pay off

    to a great author who just
    could not take it anymore

    to the often forgotten art
    of doing things the way
    they ought to be done

    and to our love.

As we took those first sensual sips, I
glanced over at one of the vintage
typewriters along the wall. I thought
about this work of words, its lack of

returns. I thought about the beautiful
piece of work sitting there next to me,
the way she loves and wants to live life,
how these words need to pull through,
for her sake. But then, I thought of the
souls of the great writers that ghost this
fateful town—Fitzgerald, and all those
books Zelda kept him from writing.
What it cost him. What it cost us.

> Many years later at the Ritz bar,
> long after the end of the World
> War II, Georges, who is the bar
> chief now and who was the
> *chasseur* when Scott lived in Paris,
> asked me, "Papa, who was this
> Monsieur Fitzgerald that everyone
> asks me about?"

~ Hemingway
A Moveable Feast

This reminded me of the sad pain
Hemingway had heard in Gertrude
Stein's pathetic pleas for her lover not
to leave. And I grieved with Baudelaire.

O Baudelaire… going down with his heartbroken ship in a cloud of opium smoke over in another part of the city.

That's when a burst of laughter from the American idiots jerked me back into the moment, where I needed to be for both our sakes, and I took a quick gulp after a lick of salt. Yes, I'm afraid I took a gulp of a 30 € margarita. But I soon settled down. I turned to peer into the hazel eyes of my wife. It still felt strange to say wife, even in my head. Yet, it also gave me a chance to realize that it no longer caused the throat-lump of terror it once did long ago. So, I reverted to sips. I tried to keep my gaze focused on her kind eyes—instead of on my navel, where, by nature and instinct, it resides. And in them, I saw a reflection of the lightning that had struck between my temples when my heart finally forced the message through to my head…

I am happy.

Oh my God. I have pulled off the close to impossible...

I've partnered with a good soul.

I took a long, salty draw. She smiled. And I knew it would take some time before I could find a way to tell her about this. So I sat back, remembered to breathe, and when she leaned over the bar treats to carefully choose from all the goodness there, I turned to the picture on the wall and whispered, silently, "If it's all the same to you, Papa, I think I'll leave the shotgun where it is."

THE FLÂNEUR

Empathy is the nature of the
intoxication to which the flâneur
abandons himself in the crowd. He
[…] enjoys the incomparable
privilege of being himself and
someone else as he sees fit. Like a
roving soul in search of a body, he
enters another person whenever he
wishes.

~ Walter Benjamin

I'm a walker. But there's more to it than
that. I'm a roamer. And I don't mean of
great wilderness distances. Though,
that's a wonderful vocation as well.

The solitary and thoughtful
stroller finds a singular
intoxication in this universal
communion.

> ~ Baudelaire
> "Crowds"
> *Paris Spleen*

I mean that I love a great city. And I
love a good ambulatory crowd of fellow
struggling souls snaking its way down
sidewalks, along the streets and alleys,
in and out of doors, or parked on the
patios of cafés.

> It is not given to every man to
> take a bath of multitude; enjoying
> a crowd is an art; and only he
> can relish a debauch of vitality at
> the expense of the human species.

> ~ Baudelaire

So, I'm an urban wanderer. Sometimes
to charge the battery of my psyche.

Sometimes to leach material from the masses. No. I suppose it's always both. So maybe I'm more of a voyeur floating around inside Baudelaire's "bath of multitude." But whatever the label, I reel from the story told in each face that passes, the history behind his peculiar gait, the heartbreak in her posture. The ever-changing scene lures me onward and into, as if the source of the Siren song were always just around the next corner. Yes, I am the one this poet of Paris sings of…

> …on whom, in his cradle, a fairy
> has bestowed the love of masks
> and masquerading, the hate of
> home, and the passion for
> roaming.

> ~ Baudelaire

Though, it's not so much a hate of home, for me, as it is some invisible mark on my forehead that gives me a jittery soul—a tattoo left by a drunk angel. More than three or four weeks in the same place, and my right shoulder begins to twitch. I can't sit still. And my ability to sleep hits the road, in hopes that I will follow.

Ashley is the one who pays the price. But she's loved me for four years now. She knows the tick and the tock of the broken clock in my head. She waves me out the door when I leave, and then wraps the most perfect set of freckled arms around me when I get back. The woman moors my flaws in the quiet harbor of her better heart, and I did not know, until my pen hit this page, that I did not understand the meaning of indebtedness.

> Multitude, solitude: identical terms, and interchangeable by the active and fertile poet.

> ~ Baudelaire

I've always felt perfectly alone in a crowded coffeehouse. I've always walked in a cloud of seclusion while dodging a thousand pedestrians in a city of millions. I project a subtle force-field around me that absorbs their energies and afflictions. And then I burn to sit at a small, preferably candlelit, table and write about what they shot me full of. If it sounds like hell to you, that's fine. Means more candlelit tables for me.

> The man who is unable to people his solitude is equally unable to be alone in a bustling crowd.

> ~ Baudelaire

Maybe Emily Dickinson was able to people her profound solitude. Maybe she peopled it more with bees and horses than she did people. Maybe a few other writers have successfully written from a vacuum of human and physical interaction with the world. I'd say most of them didn't. I would ask,

Where is the literary grease on a soul that carefully shielded itself from the blood and sex of life out in the arena?

Now, I do loves me a good cabin in the woods, or beach house in the sun, for editing a book. But the writing arrives, without fail, from a solitary immersion in the bustling crowd. And, yes, maybe Gary Snyder pulled off peopling his poems with mountains, meadows, and the Latinate names for every plant and animal known to science. But, most others who have tried, shouldn't have.

Wow. Aren't I an opinionated s.o.b? I'm only saying, if someone wants to write to me of Paris, I'd like to smell the soles of a thousand shoes splashing in filthy puddles along the Rue de Rivoli. I want to know he stuck his nose down close enough to the River Seine to catch a whiff of the boat fuel and the rat shit, maybe lose some of the edge on his blind romance with the city, so a truer

love can begin. I want her to touch
down at Charles de Gaulle mad in her
bookish passion for the place, and then
leave brokenhearted… but, a better
person for it.

> What men call love is a very
> small, restricted, feeble thing
> compared with this ineffable orgy,
> this divine prostitution of the soul
> giving itself entire, all its poetry
> and all its charity, to the
> unexpected as it comes along, to
> the stranger as he passes.

> ~ Baudelaire

As for me? I got close enough to smell
the boat fuel. But, I am not leaving
brokenhearted. I mean… I'm on my
honeymoon, y'all. So I ask for a little
latitude there.

4 RUE VIVIENNE

White tablecloths. Careful rows of four
empty wine glasses lined up between
place settings. Very silver ware, right
down to the small round tray that held
our bottle of Château Saint Estève. And
all of it reveled in a sodium-like orange
glow from the grand brass chandeliers
that were really more like magnificently
crafted indoor street lamps.

Monumental floral arrangements with
red, red roses in wide bloom, stood on
the bar in vases the size of megaphones.
Except, they were crystal megaphones.

So, what does a couple do for a last supper, when they come to the end of their honeymoon in France? Well, the options are legion. And for two people who suffer from a rather acute case of clinical indecision, the prospect could be debilitating. But for some reason, thank God, we just sort of knew what we wanted. Since we were back in Paris for the night, we went straight for the throat of one last grand cliché...

Le Grand Colbert.

LE GRAND SCENE

I remember the movie pretty well.
Diane Keaton sits alone in the black
leather booth. She fingers a glass of red
wine next to a white rose in a vase. She
seems moderately happy, but then spies,
through a cut-glass panel, the inimitable
Jack Nicholson stepping in through the
front door rubbing his hands together
and blowing on them... because it is
January outside. And that's why he's
wearing the long black overcoat with a
purplish-blue scarf folded ascott-style
and tucked in beneath the lapels.

She jerks up in a flash of problematic
revelation, as he goes up on tiptoes

trying to find her. And when he does, and comes to the table, she gurgles and gushes in a sense of terrified ecstasy. They pathetically bump noses, cheeks, and lips when he moves in for a kiss that never quite happens because she's in shock and not sure what will happen when the someone she's with gets back from the bathroom—that someone being Keanu Reeves, who is his usual dorky self in the role of new boyfriend, as actual acting may or may not be a part of what he does for a living. The jury's out on that one.

(And, okay, that was enough detail to rat me out. I did rent the movie and watch the scene again, after we got home, so I could fill out this brief chapter a bit. But just go with me on this one. It is such a tender moment in a movie, which is rare in the last ten to twenty years. And it is inspiring in spite of Mr. Reeves—clear evidence, I'd say, of just how incredible Jack and Diane are. And, yes, I'm being a bit hard on Keanu. But I'm a storyteller, and that's what storytellers do.)

Anyway, *Something's Gotta Give*. That's the movie. And that's why we came here on our last night in Paris. The dénouement was filmed in Le Grand Colbert right before the closing scene where they met, sans Reeves, on the Pont d' Arcole bridge.

We thought we would grab some dinner there, and then maybe meander over to some romantical bridge above the River Seine for a romantical kiss… or two.

C'mon. You'd do the same thing if you were in love.

How Could It Be?

The maître d' seated us with Parisian efficiency in the front far-left corner, our backs to a booth that looked the same as Diane Keaton's—a booth where the side wall meets the front windows. (The wary dog in me, who does not like to have anyone behind him, was very happy.) In other words, it seemed to us one of the best seats in the house. So of course I couldn't help the creeping of my inherent suspicion, as I wondered how that could have happened at the hand of yet another host bearing a deeply furrowed brow and a demonstrative disinterest in our existence. There we sat, nonetheless.

Our waitress appeared to lean the same way until Ashley had the wherewithal to ask her, about twenty minutes in, if she ever gets tired of stupid tourists who come here because of the silly movie.

"Yes," she said, and then smiled for the first time. So, we laughed and left it at that for the night, which she seemed to appreciate even more. Ergo, our service continued to improve in the wake of our silence on the cinematic matter.

ECSTASY D' OIGNON

Ashley ordered a Sapphire Gin apéritif because, as we are continuing to learn over here, a person is supposed to have at least one drink before the meal, a few during, and one to two after. The thing that arrived next, though, topped every other thing we ordered for the rest of the evening. For me, it topped most of the dishes we'd shared over the entire trip… the *Soupe a l' Oignon Gratinée.*

I hear what you may or may not be saying, *Well yeah, to order French onion soup here—in France—would seem like a safe move.* But this… this was more than the French getting something right that they should get right because it was named in their honor. This...

...this, to begin with, landed on the table like some breathlessly-executed touchdown of a lunar module. The care and precision with which our waitress lowered it to the cloth made it seem almost as important, and that she was pleased we had ordered it.

It came in a white porcelain bowl fired to a white porcelain base, making the two-piece apparatus the size of a small garden planter. The bubbly blanket of hot white cheese covering the top was lightly burnt to perfection, so thick it formed a seal over the soup. It had even overflowed and was stuck in crusty gold waves all down the sides to the base, like a gurgling albino volcano.

Once we broke through, which took some doing, we discovered big meaty chunks of baguette swimming in a deep pool of caramelized onions and beef and bone stock. And, I am certain, more ambrosial things than that.

I'm getting a little choked up here...

It amazes me the poet Pablo Neruda wrote an ode only to the onion itself, and not to this pot of gilded vegetable goodness, among his many hymns to the fruits of the earth that grace our tables. I can only believe that it was because he never had it. And though I won't attempt an ode here, something, at the least, must be said.

What will make this difficult, however, is that the superlative case makes me very nervous as a writer—by claiming something for its object that is tough to prove. So, being careful to use no word like "mostest," I will instead say, this was a real "discovering Victoria Falls" sort of moment.

Wait. That's a bad comparison. I didn't discover Le Grand Colbert's Oignon Gratinée any more than Dr. Livingstone discovered Victoria Falls—considering the Kololo people had already lived in South Africa for who knows how many ages. Therefore, I will back up, give up, and just commit the literary sin anyway:

This... was... the best... bowl of
freaking French onion soup
I have ever... had.

There. It is done.

Uh Oh . . .

That first time the woman in the couple sitting next to you in a fine restaurant speaks, or asks a question—and in restaurants it's usually the woman, whereas in bars it's usually the man, especially if he's not in a couple—my immediate reaction is, *Oh dear God... please... no.* And I'm lucky when I only say it in my head.

But this couple seemed so in love. Not the silly kind. More the kind that says, *We are adults now... and we can contain ourselves, somewhat.* They did kiss a few times. But this is Paris. And two lovers kissing in Paris is like dogs sleeping in dusty driveways in the small towns of Oklahoma. Ain't nobody gonna think nothin' of it.

So when the first words came—and, to be truthful, I can't actually remember which one spoke them—there was an ease to the launch of the conversation. They are Parisiens who had never been to Le Grand Colbert and thought it was time to give it a try. We are "from the States… Oklahoma," we told them, because overseas you don't ever just say "Oklahoma," unless you enjoy blank stares. For that matter, this is not only required overseas. I find I still have to introduce myself the same way when in places like Maine, or Idaho. But we also mentioned we were on our honeymoon, and they got excited about that.

They sipped on their glasses of white, as we sipped on our red, and we made it as far as their confession that they didn't feel like they would be welcome there in

Oklahoma, because Americans don't really like the French lately. I assured them they were wrong, and especially when it comes to Oklahoma. "Hell," I said, "with those accents, as long as you don't work for the French government, folks would fight over who gets to host you for dinner every night." Which is mostly true. (Of course, it's not like we'd take them down to Durant, or say, Ada, where they throw people in jail for all manner of things besides being guilty of an actual crime.)

> Strap them kids in.
> Give 'em a little bit o' vodka
> in a Cherry Coke.
> We're goin' to Oklahoma
>
> ~ James McMurtry
> "Choctaw Bingo"

After a little more fun and a few laughs, we all decided it was time to turn our attentions back to the wonderful food before us. Ashley enjoyed her skate fish with capers. I'm pretty sure I liked my brochette, but that damn onion soup messed me up to the point I can't quite focus or remember. At the same time, somewhere in the middle of all this, we began to realize the gin and the wine were having a more profound effect on Ashley than usual.

UH OH . . . PART DEUX

At first, her eyes had trouble focusing
on the food and silverware. She had
switched to drinking water. But soon
she was needing to steady herself by
holding on to my arm and leaning
against me. And that is when... the
two full flutes of champagne arrived.

Our waitress graciously gestured that
our nice new friends next to us had
ordered them as a gift in honor of our
honeymoon. They looked over, smiled,
and raised their glasses. I helped Ashley
to locate her flute. We raised ours and
smiled back our best gratitude. We all
sipped. Only, Ashley pretended. I then

voiced our thanks. There was some talk. They were so sweet. And yet, now… we had a problem, Houston. A big, serious problem. Or, more like two little bubbly problems, sitting there on our table.

Ashley gives out the quietest and cutest faint traces of a whimper when she knows she's in drink-related trouble. It's very rare for her. But when I hear them, I know it is time to put on the Captain America cape. So, I started to reach over, when the couple wasn't looking, and draw healthy swigs of Ashley's champagne, and then set it back down in front of her. Meanwhile, I continued to sip on mine. We couldn't let them down. We couldn't just up and leave the gift untouched like yet another pair of culturally-insensitive tourists from America. We had our country to think of. So they'd look away. I'd swig. They'd glance back. We'd smile. I'd sip mine… swig hers… and repeat.

As we neared the bottoms of our two little problems, I paid and thanked our waitress. Then I mouthed to Ashley to hold on tight. I assured her that all we needed to do was make it to and out the door. From there, we'd be home free. A couple of drunks stumbling around in love on the streets of Paris would not be any more unusual than a couple kissing in a restaurant. And they've been putting up with drunk poets here for centuries. *Just give it your best shot*, I whispered, *at thanking our friends as we slip by. I will go overboard to cover for you. And we can do this, Baby. You ready?*

She nodded. I slammed what was left of the little problems, then helped her up, and held on tight, as did she. We made our thanks. They again congratulated. Everyone waved and goodbyed. And we were out the door of Le Grand Colbert without even a stumble… nor a minute to spare.

Uh Oh . . . Part Trois

We wobbled our tipsy way down Rue
Vivienne, but from there on, the street
names didn't play much of a role in the
rest of the evening. We wandered in,
out, and around the Palais Royal. (I
believe.) And somewhere among those
vaulted arcades my woozy head stopped
communicating with my feet as well as
it had been when we left the restaurant.

It took no time to figure out that I was
not going to get off scot-free for having
slammed two glasses of champagne at
the back end of our shared bottle of
red. I don't think I whimpered. I want
to believe I didn't, at least. But I did

look over at Ashley with small flashes of desperation in my eyes. I now had to think through the individual steps of walking. Something that came naturally on most days. The instructions played out in my head:

Which foot comes next? … Help!
The one that's behind you, you moron…

And on and on it went for a while. But, as minor miracles would have it, Ashley began to rebound right about the same time. So, we simply shifted who was leaning upon whom and continued on our way back in the general direction of the river. The whole thing came off like a questionable covert operation that we executed flawlessly. And just before I recovered, which I eventually did as we neared the Seine, I thought I heard the ghost of Napoleon telling me he was impressed. And that he could've used us at the Battle of Waterloo.

EAU . . . AAAAH . . .

As everyone knows, meditation
and water are wedded forever.

~ Herman Melville
Moby Dick

What is it that water does to me?

Why does my soul sing, like a child
straddle-legged on the floor with a new
toy, when I come into its presence?

I love the monastic echoes that bounce
off its stillness in an alpine pond. I also
love the piratic gut-laugh that roars up
out of the rage of its waves on the

ocean's shore—the brooding ocean, so temperamental and so deadly between its bouts of gargantuan silence and depression.

But the river—albeit no stranger to times of stillness and rage—is the brooding philosopher flowing in a constant question about what it means to be moving—whether you are an air-breather with legs, a clock with arms, or a water molecule evaporating into the atmosphere, falling into the mountains, then spilling, bumping, and rolling your way to the sea.

Does all our human motion matter? Is it just something a harried God gave us to do, like a parent telling the kids to go play in the traffic so he can have a good stiff drink?

I don't know. And I don't know if the river knows either. Though I do believe that water goes about its occupation with considerably less whining, less bitching, and less disorganization than humans. Maybe that's why I love the water so much. And, especially, its philosopher, the river. I respect its diligence and commitment, and the wisdom that must have come with its incredible age.

So maybe that's why I stood dazed at the dark rail of the Pont d' Arts Bridge, staring down at the midnight waters of the Seine for long enough that Ashley had to poke me and remind me that I had come to Paris with her, not the river.

Of course, it also could've been the stream of wine and champagne I had stuck my head in at dinner continuing to have its way with me.

ADIEU

I know—the city no longer holds
secrets. But there are plane trees,
squares, cafés, friendly streets, and
the bright gaze of clouds that
slowly dies.

> ~ Adam Zagajewski
> "Luxembourg Gardens"
> *Unseen Hand*

We had stumbled onto the ritual of
what goes on at the Pont d' Arts bridge
the night before we left for Bordeaux.
After our dinner at Brasserie Lipp, we
wandered along some back streets of
the Latin Quarter, with no particular
aim, and eventually came around from

behind the Bibliothèque Mazarine. That was when we heard the gentle buzz of laughter and life on the bridge, long before we saw it.

Pont d' Arts is a pedestrian affair, so it's a great spot for young people to drink, snack, and mingle—but mostly drink—in the heart of Paris without the fear of a double-decker bus, a motorcycle, a cop, or a car running them down in their shoes and then fleeing the scene. The party heats up after the sun goes down, and by midnight you can barely make it from one end to the other without bumping into a musician or falling into someone's cheese and wine spread out on a blanket right in the middle of the whole lovely mess.

And because of the press of flesh, it's also hard to miss the guy who walks back and forth with a silver bucket of wine and beer sitting on ice. That first time, we'd bought a bottle of rosé for ten euros, had him open it, then sat with our backs to the railing and took turns tipping it back. Looking around us, it was obvious that glassware was optional. Tonight though, we thought it best to let him walk on by. We were tired and tipsy and had only come to say goodbye to France. So, for a while, we looked out on the burning glow of the dinner boats floating toward and then under us. White beams of light would shoot up between the wooden planks, glinting off bottles and making the water below look like a shatter of trinkets and baubles.

We also contemplated the hundreds of padlocks that people had hooked and locked into the mesh of chain-link fence that spanned the rails on both sides of the bridge. We learned later it has to do with lovers who attach them and then throw the key into the river, sealing their bond forever—a grandiose gesture committed by the young and the feverish… or maybe the old and the very forgetful. I would fall in the latter category I guess. That's why I wish we'd had a padlock with us.

Grandiose gestures aside, how do I explain the way this place makes me feel? It's something in the dried blood of all the artists who've lived and died here. It's the sigh and groan of a city that clocks in as "ancient," as opposed to just old. It's in the way the young people sit there on the bridge talking and laughing face to face for hours, as opposed to through a screen. Like a friend of mine once said, "It was like a real life Facebook!" And because I love him, I didn't say, "Well, imagine *that*…" while nodding my head.

It's these things, as well as the human tempest that blasts its way through the streets, parks, and the cafés every day, raining down love, beauty, and light… as well as the hopeless desperation and

violence hidden among the shadows…
that enchants anyone who is willing to
swim in the sotted run-off of it all.

It's a profane dream.

It's an elegant nightmare.

I would not live here.

But, I will visit every time
someone's got an extra ticket.

THE BEACON

You know you're headed back to the
center of the United States when…

you've jerked up out of bed at 6:00 a.m.
after five hours of sleep and too much
champagne the night before, then just
barely survived an overpriced taxi ride
to the Charles de Gaulle International
Airport, where you maintained your
composure when the agent pulled you
out of the security line for an extended
violation of your personal belongings,
but have, finally, made it to the last
couple of chairs available at the gate
next door to the one you want, so you
do, at least, feel a certain confidence

that you will be getting on the plane
bound for Texas, and then…

you see it:

the extraordinary mass of blond hair
bricked up as high as the apprentice
hairdresser could reach on her little
plastic footstool…

the orange canned-tan smashed into a
pair of ripped stone-washed designer
jeans with silver crosses stitched on the
back pockets…

and the black silk tour jacket with
nothing but **JESUS** spanning the
entire back of it in bright, blaring,
pearly-white letters.

For God's Sake,
as Well as Yours

Next time, think it through…

I know. You'd planned for years. You
had both dreamed of going to France.
Things came up. Not the least of which
was a precious little boy who's now set
on cruise control through the agitated
wasteland of his terrible twos. And, for
some reason that can only be pondered
by psychologists who study the aberrant
brains of young parents, you decide—
against the mountains of evidence and
centuries of good advice from other
parents who have gone before you—
that it's now time to fulfill the fantasy

of your foreign getaway. Besides, just think of the cultural osmosis that would permeate that little guy's mind with the stuff of art, literature, and the history of Europe's gruesome wars.

And, consider not what the airbus's ascent will inflict on his tiny eustachian tubes—the painful pressure you will not be able to explain to him how to pop—nor the extreme discomfort he'll surely experience at the hands of eleven solid hours strapped into his car seat that no amount of cookies and sippy cups will assuage. For that matter, why bother about the emotionally mind-splitting stress and excruciating agitation that his incessant whining and crying will cause us, the passengers in the 40 to 50 rows before, aft, and around you, until they finally die down to steady waves of whimpering moans. That is, until the descent when we'll all return to the Ninth Circle of Hell together.

And, I have not even touched on the weeping and gnashing of teeth this will cause you as you begin to think back on how peaceful and whimsical your lives were before he came along—how easy things used to be. And this will make you feel even worser and awfuler as a parent. You'll begin to question your qualifications. And then… you will contemplate scratching your own eyeballs out in a sad hope for some sympathy from the couple in seats E and F. But they won't give it. And you will then be blind for no good reason.

Yet… alas… if you simply must travel overseas with a toddler… please…

please consider the last verse of McMurtry's "Choctaw Bingo":

> *Give 'em a little bit o' Benadryl*
> *in a Cherry Coke.*

Arrivals and Departures

The plane bumps and bobbles on the last leg from Houston to Oklahoma City. A much smaller one. Two seats per side. And the reason for our trip sleeps in the one next to me. "The honeymoon is over…" but only in the literal sense. As a euphemism, it was over a long time ago for me.

Wait. That sounds bad. I meant to say, where the "concept" of honeymoons is concerned, I no longer harbor the usual delusions of youth. But, do I love this woman? Yes. Did I want to marry her? No question. Still, those two things do not always go together, historically. So, what I want made clear is that she is, to me, far more than love and marriage. She is a good, radically kind, and deeply sensitive soul... a genetic anomaly that on darker days I fear, with every passing year, occurs less and less in the human DNA structure. The thought of that worries me as much or more as the instability of these go-cart-sized twin-engine tuna cans with wings.

But here we are, at the end of the honeymoon ride. And, in the great rodeo of life back down on earth, I'm afraid I will be a wild ride for her. So I offer my sympathies, and apologies, in advance. No one's used enough rosin and hung onto the rope for the full eight seconds with me yet. But this woman is a strong one...
and loves animals.

A Cold Pleasure

Looking back on the trip now, these
words from Adam Zagajewski sum up a
strange something about Paris for me:

Foreignness is splendid,
a cold pleasure.
Yellow lights illuminate
the windows on the Seine
(there's the real mystery:
the life of others).

~ Adam Zagajewski
"Luxembourg Gardens"
Unseen Hand

It's a strange something I haven't been able to wrap up with a red bow yet, but I've got the paper and Scotch tape:

Paris will tolerate a visit. But it prefers you not stay. The yellow glow in those boathouse windows entices, but it will not invite you in. And those curtains remain open only to torture your foreignness.

Still, I enjoyed walking there on the quai. The cold pleasure of it was splendid. And like the waters of the Seine, all of us are passing on our way to somewhere else… a somewhere else Paris hopes we'll get to soon… and a somewhere else most want to get back to, but not before we've spent the full amount of our cold pleasure…

and not before we've taken the time we need to bathe in the glow and the real mystery of the life of others.

Author Bio

Nathan Brown is an author, songwriter, and award-winning poet living in Wimberley, Texas. He holds a PhD in English and Journalism from the University of Oklahoma and taught there for over twenty years. He also served as Poet Laureate for the State of Oklahoma in 2013 and 2014.

He's published roughly 20 books. Among them is *Don't Try*, a collection of poems co-written with songwriter and Austin Music Hall-of-Famer, Jon Dee Graham. His *Oklahoma Poems, and Their Poets* anthology was a finalist for the Oklahoma Book Award. *Karma Crisis: New and Selected Poems* was a finalist for the Paterson Poetry Prize and the Oklahoma Book Award. His earlier book, *Two Tables Over*, won the 2009 Oklahoma Book Award. He has also released several CDs of original music.

For more, go to: **brownlines.com**

MEZCALITA
PRESS

An independent publishing company dedicated to bringing the printed poetry, fiction, and non-fiction of musicians who want to add to the power and reach of their important cultural voices.

Visit us at: www.mezpress.com